D0295819

CANCELLED

The Dog Rescuers

www.penguin.co.uk

The Dog Rescuers

HEARTWARMING TRUE 'TAILS' OF RESCUE, RECOVERY AND RE-HOMING

With a foreword by RSPCA
Inspector Anthony Joynes

BANTAM PRESS

LONDON · NEW YORK · TORONTO · SYDNEY · AUCKLAND

TRANSWORLD PUBLISHERS
61–63 Uxbridge Road, London W5 5SA
www.penguin.co.uk

Transworld is part of the Penguin Random House group of companies
whose addresses can be found at global.penguinrandomhouse.com

First published in Great Britain in 2018 by Bantam Press
an imprint of Transworld Publishers

A CIP catalogue record for this book
is available from the British Library.

ISBN
9780593080405

Types_____ in 11.75/14.5pt Bembo MT by Jouve (UK), Milton Keynes.
Print_____ ____ bound in Great Britain by Clays Ltd, Elcograf S.p.A.

fut____ ___ ___ business, our readers and our planet. This book
is ___ ____ from Forest Stewardship Council®

Contents

Foreword by RSPCA Inspector Anthony Joynes

I'VE BEEN an RSPCA inspector for more than nine years, and it's the best job in the world. Every day, I and the other 320 inspectors make a difference to the lives of abused and neglected animals, intervening to give them the futures they deserve and need.

Of course, it's incredibly frustrating at times, and sometimes very sad, and I've spent many sleepless nights worrying about animals whose suffering has really got to me and almost broken my heart. It's not a nine-to-five job, one that you can leave at the door at the end of the day. I'm lucky that I have a very supportive family – my girlfriend, Georgia, and my son, Caleb – as well as our own rescue dog, Bella. They help me to switch off, which isn't always easy because I feel so passionately about the dogs and other animals I deal with.

When I'm on duty I know that I always achieve something, whether it's giving the smallest piece of advice to an owner in order to make an animal's life better, or taking action to rescue an animal from the most terrible circumstances imaginable. In my work I see dogs who've been subjected to appalling torture, forced to fight, neglected and starved to the point of death; images that stay with you. I've seen the worst of humanity – the owners who carry out these atrocities.

However, I've also watched as terrified, shivering and whimpering dogs have been brought back to full health and happy lives through skilled veterinary and behavioural treatment and large amounts of tender loving care. I've seen nervous and aggressive dogs gradually learn to trust human beings again, when everything in their past has taught them to expect nothing but savage cruelty. Best of all, I've seen animals that have known months and years of misery re-homed with families and owners who give them all the love, companionship and care they deserve.

My job, however terrible at times, is one of hope. I may meet people who've inflicted appalling cruelty on animals, but I also meet the staff at the animal centres, the dedicated foster carers, the vets who go above and beyond their duty for these suffering animals, and the new owners who take them on and give them forever homes. All these people are amazing and it's a privilege to work alongside them.

Every year, 130,000 animals are rescued by the RSPCA — 7,669 of which were dogs in 2017 — and our call centre deals with more than a million calls every year from concerned members of the public. The RSPCA is the oldest animal charity in the world, dedicated to looking after animals since 1824, so I'm following in a proud tradition.

For as long as I can remember, it's been my dream to do this amazing job. My childhood nickname, given to me by my mum and my stepdad, was Dr Dolittle, because I always seemed more interested in animals than anything else, including humans. Our house, on a council estate close to Tranmere Rovers' football ground in Birkenhead, was always home to animals: rabbits, cats, and a dog called Sandy, who was my closest childhood friend.

One of my earliest memories, from when I was about five, is of seeing a man in our street kick a dog, and my mum going for him and giving him the sharp edge of her tongue.

I was too young to properly understand why I felt so proud of what she did, but the way she stood up for that defenceless animal could be what started the ball rolling for me.

Animals large and small always held great interest for me. Whenever I'd go out fishing with my stepdad I'd take birdseed along with us, and spent most of the time coaxing chaffinches to feed from my hand. I'd bought the seed with my friend Gary, who lived opposite me, and we spent the rest of our saved-up pocket money making bird-feeders to put in our gardens.

When we were about eight or nine, he and I also set up our own animal rescue service, going round the neighbourhood looking for injured animals. A year or so later, when I was around ten, I used to go to a youth club at the bottom of our road, where all the local kids went to play football and snooker. I became a regular there, five nights a week, kicking a ball around with my mates. One evening, close to Bonfire Night, I saw that some older lads, who must have been thirteen or fourteen, had caught a duck (a female mallard) and were trying to attach a firework to her with duct tape. I felt a boiling rage as I watched them and, despite the fact that they were older and bigger, I barged into the middle of their group, grabbed the duck and ran home with her as fast as I could. Mum helped me remove the tape and we put the duck into an empty rabbit hutch for the night, because it was too dark to free her immediately. The next morning we took her to Birkenhead Park, released her, and thankfully she flew on to the pond, safe and well.

I got a lot of stick from other kids at the youth club for what I did, but I was quite tough and I refused to let them intimidate me. I just had an overriding feeling that I'd done the right thing, and it's the same feeling I get doing my job today, even when I have to stand up to some quite intimidating individuals in the course of things.

It was a couple of years after that incident that I encountered first-hand the work of the RSPCA. About five doors away from us lived a Dobermann and his owner. I never saw the dog being walked, but whenever me and my mates were playing football in the field behind his house we'd hear him barking. He sounded really unhappy. He must have slipped out through the gate one day, because I saw him making his way along the road, emaciated and, apparently, delirious. He was staggering badly and kept bumping into parked cars. The owner came out and coaxed him back to the house, but I shouted to him: 'Your dog's ill, it needs to see a vet.' He ignored me and took the dog back inside.

I immediately went back home and rang the RSPCA cruelty line. The operator assured me that my details wouldn't be passed on to the owner, but I didn't care if they were. I wanted the owner to face the consequences of his actions and inactions, and I was proud that I'd done something to make that happen. Mostly, I just wanted that dog to be well again.

A couple of hours later I saw the RSPCA van arrive and a female officer went into the house. I had my nose pressed against the glass of our front window, even though Mum kept telling me to get away. About half an hour later the RSPCA inspector came out with the dog wrapped in a big towel. He probably had to be put to sleep; he was in such a bad way. I felt so sad for him, but even at that age I knew it was better than for him to be suffering. So I also felt energized, realizing that there's someone you can call to protect animals, and they really will do something.

During my teenage years the only other thing that mattered to me, almost as much as animals, was football. I wanted to play professionally, and I had trials for Tranmere Rovers and Chester City, but eventually I had to face the fact that I wasn't good enough. Luckily, I'd worked hard enough at school to get good A levels. I went to Liverpool John Moores University and did a degree in biomedical sciences, largely because I was good at science and when I'd read about it in the prospectus it had sounded interesting, but also because I knew it was a subject that would lead to a job.

Halfway through the course, I realized that I didn't want to work in a laboratory five days a week, testing blood and tissue samples. I wanted to work with animals. When I finished my degree I wrote to Chester Zoo, but they told me I was overqualified for any vacancies they had. So I did what lots of newly qualified students do: I went travelling for six months and came back with greater energy and focus.

On my return home I saw that the RSPCA was recruiting for the Inspectorate, so I – and 4,000 others – applied for the twenty-four jobs that were going. I was convinced I wouldn't get in, so I also applied to do a PGCE (a Postgraduate Certificate in Education), which would have led to a career in teaching.

Ever since the formation of the RSPCA, its Inspectorate has investigated animal welfare concerns, collecting and rescuing animals that may be suffering. Inspectors are trained and equipped to enforce serious breaches of legislation by using Improvement Notices and, if necessary, formal case investigations, which may result in judicial proceedings.

It's a job that comes with a great deal of responsibility and it's unsurprising that the selection process is rigorous. Initially, I went on a selection day with about sixteen other applicants. We were given tasks to do – constructing a paper bridge strong enough to hold a bar of chocolate, for instance – and, as I'm not very practical (I should never be let loose with a hammer and nails), I was sure I'd failed. Of course, they weren't looking for DIY skills, but at how the candidates interacted with one another; who demonstrated good communication skills and personable qualities.

After some other tests, I was amazed to learn I'd made the shortlist of 150 applicants, and was invited to the RSPCA headquarters near Horsham in West Sussex for two days of further assessments. The physical fitness test was no problem, but I felt that all the other interviews and tests were disasters, and that the assessors probably thought that, at twenty-two years old, I was just too young. I left Horsham deflated, sure that I was going to be a science teacher instead.

It was summer 2008 as I awaited the letter from the RSPCA telling me whether I'd made the cut. Someone had told me that if it was a fail, the letter would come in a normal-sized envelope, and say thanks but no thanks, but if I'd passed, it would be a large packet full of forms and details. In August I went away with some friends to V Festival in Staffordshire and the weather was so bad – torrential rain – that my phone got soaked through the pocket of my jeans. The battery was almost flat – I could get it to work for a few seconds, then it went dead – so when Mum rang to say I'd had a letter through the post, I shouted, 'Is it thin or thick?' before the phone cut out. I had to borrow a mate's phone and move away from the crowds to hear anything. When I got through, my mum and sister were both screaming excitedly, 'It's a pack, it's a thick pack!'

Mum asked me if I wanted her to open it and read it. At first I said no, then I realized I wouldn't be able to relax until I knew for sure. So she ripped the package open and read out the best words I'd ever heard: 'We are pleased to offer you the role of inspector.'

The training took a year, and was rigorous. Early on we had to learn how to euthanize a large animal humanely, because that's something an inspector may be called on to do if a horse or a deer, or another large animal, is badly injured, or if a trailer full of cattle and pigs has overturned on a motorway and the animals are both in danger and causing danger. We were taken to an abattoir and, although I wasn't looking forward to it, I was determined to learn how to do the deed quickly, humanely and efficiently. Since I qualified I've never had to put that aspect of my training to the test, thankfully, but I'm prepared. You never know when those skills will be needed.

I was sent on two different field placements during that year of training. The first was in beautiful, rural Much Wenlock in Shropshire, where I was based at a wildlife sanctuary. I'd be out all day with the chief inspector, who was teaching me the job, and then at night I'd be feeding bats and fox cubs at the sanctuary. The other placement was a complete contrast, in a busy area of the North East, dealing with lots of cases of cruelty and neglect.

When I qualified I was initially posted to North Wales, commuting from Mum's house on the Wirral, before I transferred to the area I now cover in the North West. I always dreamed of working where I grew up, and I'm now responding to cruelty against animals in a professional capacity in the same area where, as a boy, I ran my own animal rescue club.

It's one of the busiest areas in England for the RSPCA. There are twelve inspectors in the group covering the Wirral, Cheshire, part of Greater Manchester and a little bit of Derbyshire. Many of the complaints we get from the public are concerns about animals left out in gardens without shelter, that sort of thing – but I never know when I start a shift what I will face that day, and it may be a case of extreme neglect or appalling cruelty. We get many more calls in spring and summer, because the days are longer and people are outside more, so they simply see more. There are lots of calls about injured wildlife, and lots of problems to do with the casual neglect of pets.

In most reported concerns, all the owner needs is some advice and support to bring their pet back to full health and happiness. Caring for an animal takes commitment, time and energy, and sometimes owners are genuinely overwhelmed by other problems in their lives, so the care of their pet can sometimes fall through the cracks. Some owners take on a dog or a cat, with no real knowledge of how to feed or exercise them, or when to seek appropriate veterinary care, and my job is to give these people information and encouragement. However, on occasion, an animal has been so badly neglected that we have no other option but to take it away. That's an extremely difficult situation to handle, but again, that's when the training and knowledge of the law kicks in.

Each year I deal with perhaps five or six cases where an animal has suffered a non-accidental injury: in other words, it has been the victim of deliberate cruelty. These are the worst cases I see, because the culprits are often callous, savage brutes, and I struggle to understand their behaviour. I work with the police, and follow the case as it reaches the magistrates' court if the RSPCA decides to prosecute and the perpetrator goes to court. It's a tough part of my job, but also one of the most satisfying, especially if the animal is rescued in time for them to be rehabilitated and given a new future.

On one occasion, I had to go to HMP Liverpool to interview a man accused of domestic violence, which included animal cruelty. He'd been brutally assaulting his partner, and when the dog tried to protect her he poured boiling water on it. As I was questioning him in a prison cubicle, I became aware of someone watching me. I looked up, and it was the guy who'd been kicking the dog in our street, all those years ago. We didn't acknowledge each other, but I could tell he knew who I was. I almost welled up, thinking,

'Look where you are now, and look where I am.' I have no idea why he was there, but I feel passionately that we need to take the relationship between animal cruelty and other crimes very seriously: just read Ruby's story on page 203 and you'll see what I mean.

As RSPCA inspectors, we don't work in isolation. I start the process, by taking a broken dog away from terrible cruelty or neglect, but after I've done my bit, a lot of other dedicated people are also involved. There are vets who work at reduced rates for the RSPCA, because we are a charity and don't have infinite resources. These vets are sometimes called out to help me and the police take a dog into possession, and they often do it in their spare time. Then there are the dedicated staff and volunteers at the animal centres, who give all the special care and love that these abused animals need to help them flourish and find new homes. It's a delight to know that in 2017 alone, 8,893 rescued dogs were successfully re-homed. The many people who help make this happen go above and beyond their job descriptions, day after day.

There are also specialists in animal behaviour who work with the dogs to rehabilitate them and bring their behaviour up to the standard necessary for them to be re-homed successfully. The fosterers are amazing too, taking on dogs who are in a bad way, mentally or physically, and giving them the chance of a fresh start. Everything would crash down around our heads without the foster carers, and I admit I can often be cheeky when dealing with them, persuading people to foster a dog I know needs help, playing on the goodness of their hearts, hoping against hope that they simply won't be able to refuse.

I don't feel guilty, though, because looking after a dog is always a two-way street. For all the care a dog is given, it will give back in love and affection. Playing with dogs is wonderful therapy, the most uplifting thing you can do if you're having a bad day or are under stress. I'd go as far as to say I think it should be prescribed on the NHS!

The dogs I rescue are never far from my mind. I often go to the animal centre and check on the dogs I've taken in, and there's always a truly magical moment when I see a beaten, damaged dog begin to show playfulness. It's great for them, of course – but it also makes me feel good about myself and my job. I've enriched their lives, and they've enriched mine.

The stories that follow are some of those that make everything we do as inspectors feel worthwhile, and I'm delighted that we're now sharing them with you here.

CHAPTER 1

Timmy

THE POLICEMAN standing guard by the front door warned RSPCA Inspector Anthony Joynes as he approached: 'It's pretty horrible in there. You'll need a peg for your nose.'

He wasn't exaggerating. The smell hit Anthony before he even crossed the threshold.

Anthony had been into squalid houses many times before to rescue neglected and abused animals, but even he was taken aback when he stepped inside. Even though it was October and cold, there was no heating or electricity in the house and he felt the chill straight away. Outside, there had been warning signs – an overgrown garden full of discarded junk, murky windows – but inside, the 'home' (did someone actually live here?) was piled high with rubbish: old food containers spilling out of plastic bags, abandoned junk mail strewn ankle-deep.

The powerful stench Anthony had been warned about was coming from the dog faeces that covered the floor in almost every room. There were mounds of it on every tread of the staircase; on the kitchen, bathroom and bedroom floors. Everything was covered in it, and Anthony and the two policemen with him soon gave up trying to step around it. With dog mess matted into the carpets and smeared up the walls and skirting boards, it was unavoidable. A cloud of black flies swirled above the squalor. It was disgusting, and it was disturbing.

It was the presence of the swarm of flies that had brought the police out in the first place. Firemen, out making routine visits along the road to persuade residents to fit smoke alarms, had peered through the front window of the property, seen the mounds of rubbish and the flies, and asked the next-door neighbour if they knew who lived there. Hearing that nobody had been seen at the house for weeks, they feared the worst – that there was a dead body inside – and called the police.

The police needed to break down the front door to gain entry, but there was no dead body. And that was a relief. However, cowering in the rubbish-strewn living room was a terrible sight – an elderly dog lying pathetically on the filthy sofa. At that point the dog was secured by the police, an emergency call was made to the RSPCA, and Anthony sped to the house. When the call comes in from the police, it's clear it's a serious situation.

The appalling state of the house was shocking enough, even for a man who thought he'd seen it all before, but what really made Anthony catch his breath was the enormous tumour on the side of the old dog's face. It was the size of a tennis ball, red, bloody and ulcerated, and so heavy that the poor dog's head was weighed down by it, the eye on that side of his face partly obscured and closed.

'Oh my God, what's that on your face?' Anthony asked the frightened animal, as he carefully picked his way through the debris of upended furniture and festering rubbish to reach him. The dog lay with the tumour resting on the sofa, a neglected bone next to him.

Mercifully, it was clear that the dog wasn't starving, because his body, apart from the tumour, appeared to be in quite good condition. Somebody did indeed live in the house or was, at least, stopping by regularly to give him food and water. Anthony found a washing-up bowl full of water near by, a clue that whoever was responsible for the dog was leaving it alone for long periods.

'Basic detective work told me the dog hadn't been completely abandoned,' remembers Anthony, 'as it was clear that someone had been in the house recently. But from the state of the place the dog was obviously living there alone, in the dark much of the time. No human being could live in that place.

'I checked the fridge to see if there was any food, but it was empty — thank goodness, because with no electricity anything in there would have been festering.'

The only room not plastered in faeces was the sitting room where the old dog was found.

'Bless him, he was clearly a clean animal who couldn't avoid living among the piled-up rubbish, but kept one room clear of his own mess. He didn't want to live in his own filth, poor old thing.'

As he always does in instances of neglect, Anthony took a video of the awful conditions in the house. 'Photographs don't really do justice to places like that, so I filmed all the rooms to show the sheer wretched level of squalor the sad old dog was sentenced to live in, possibly for months or even years.'

Before he could take the dog away, Anthony needed a vet to agree that the animal was suffering, or likely to suffer. Vet Holly Jones came out and instantly confirmed that the animal was suffering 'on numerous levels'. The police took possession of him and transferred him to the care of the RSPCA. They also handed over to Anthony the animal welfare investigation into the dog's owner and the cruel state in which the creature had been living.

'Everyone who'd met him – the firemen, the police, Holly and me – were keen to get him out of that disgusting place and into somewhere clean and comfortable.'

Anthony led the bewildered and apprehensive dog outside and carefully loaded him into his van. As soon as he was exposed to the world outside his squalid home for the first time in a long while, the dog was so confused and frightened that he pulled on the lead to go back inside – despite everything, the confines of the house were all he knew, and he clearly felt safe there. Adjusting to a new and better environment might take some time.

It was quite late by the time the pair arrived at the RSPCA's Wirral & Chester Branch Animal Centre, and the old fella was too agitated and unhappy for vet Holly to be able to take blood or do any other tests to assess the tumour. So she simply gave him some pain relief and antibiotics before Anthony settled him down for the night.

'I just wanted him to know that we were his friends. I didn't want him to be too stressed. He was terrified, and we wanted him to be out of pain and a bit more relaxed before Holly had a closer look at him.'

Anthony slept badly that night, waking to think about the old dog, the distressing size of the tumour, and the appalling state of the house where he'd been condemned to live alone. This was a case that really distressed him. At home, he was usually able to switch off from his routine work, but he couldn't wipe his first glimpse of the terrified animal from his mind, and he felt frustrated with the person who had left such a lovely old dog on his own in those conditions. It meant he was up early the next day, determined to track down the owner responsible.

It didn't take long. He followed leads from neighbours, and from the landlord of the house, and discovered the dog was called Timmy, he was fifteen years old and a collie cross. At this point, interviewing the owner wasn't a priority: Anthony was more concerned with getting Timmy to Holly's veterinary practice to see if anything could be done for him. The dog's welfare was foremost in his mind. Following up with the owner would have to wait.

'If the lump is cancerous,' Anthony remembers thinking, 'it may be that the best option for this old chap is to have a quiet, calm ending, with no more suffering. If he doesn't make it through today, I'll be going home wishing I'd been called six months earlier. It never comes any easier to me, no matter how long I do the job. Sometimes I know when I remove a dog from dire circumstances that the chances of them surviving and being re-homed are minute. But if there's the slightest possibility of full recovery and a new home, I'll fight for that chance.'

Despite the signs being ominous, Timmy was clearly

feeling better when Anthony saw him that morning, thanks to the painkillers, and when he was taken to the vet he enjoyed being outside – a sharp contrast to the previous day – pausing to sniff around some fuchsias.

Anthony let him enjoy the moment. 'He probably hadn't had the chance for a little sniff for ages. He'd been cooped up in that awful house for so long.'

The huge tumour was the most obvious of Timmy's problems, but not the only one. There was no evidence of live fleas, but he'd clearly had untreated fleas at some point in the past. One of his legs was caked in dried blood from where he'd been scratching, and there was fur loss around his bottom, possibly caused by the griminess of the place he'd been living in.

Holly, like Anthony, had been thinking about poor old Timmy overnight, and she came in to the practice on her day off to see if the tumour could be safely removed. She could tell it was ulcerated and infected, and that it was pulling his eye down.

'He's very lucky not to have maggots in it,' she told Anthony. 'If those flies had laid eggs in his tumour, he'd have been eaten alive by maggots.'

It didn't bear thinking about. She explained that she was going to sedate Timmy to take an X-ray of his skull. If the tumour was attached to the bone, there would be little hope for her patient. It would be too difficult to remove without taking away a large part of his jaw and cheekbone, and this just wasn't an option for a dog as old as Timmy. She also planned to X-ray his chest, to check if the cancer had spread there.

As the needle for the anaesthetic went in, Timmy released a huge, heart-rending howl of pain, and Anthony's eyes filled with sympathetic tears. Then Timmy's body relaxed as he slipped into a deep, pain-free sleep, which must have been a wonderful release for him. Anthony, too, shared the relief: whatever the outcome of the treatment, Timmy was out of pain right now, probably for the first time in weeks.

The news from the first X-ray was good: the tumour was all in the tissue and not attached to Timmy's skull. Nonetheless, Anthony and the team working on Timmy still faced an anxious wait for the results of the chest X-ray. When they finally came through, Holly showed the plates to Anthony, explaining that there were some shadows over Timmy's heart. However, these were normal for a dog of his advanced years. To everyone's relief, the cancer had not spread.

They had successfully cleared the first hurdle and there was a small sense of elation. However, Holly wisely cautioned Anthony that the major surgery she now needed to carry out to remove the tumour was particularly risky because of Timmy's age, and the amount of time he spent under anaesthetic would be crucial. It needed to be minimized, and as he'd already been under for some time while the X-rays were carried out, she would need to work quickly. She set to straight away.

'We'll get rid of this horrible, ulcerated mass that's causing him so much discomfort,' she said determinedly. 'He's had it on his face for long enough.'

She faced a difficult job, though. There wasn't much free skin on the affected side of Timmy's face, and the tumour was perilously close to his eye and lips. It was all very delicate work. A further risk was that of bleeding, as the area contained a lot of blood vessels, which had to be methodically clamped off as Holly slowly and carefully cut away at the base of the mass.

When the enormous lump eventually dropped into the waiting stainless-steel dish, Anthony felt a huge swell of optimism, realizing Timmy's odds had improved significantly. He put on surgical gloves and picked up the tumour: 'I couldn't believe how heavy it was, and he'd been living with it attached to him. It must have been agony.'

Despite the good news, because of his advancing years Timmy wasn't yet out of the woods, and he spent the following twenty-four hours being closely monitored at the veterinary practice. Holly had delicately stitched the laceration to give Timmy the best possible cosmetic result, but in those early days the large wound reminded Anthony of The Joker's smile.

'Timmy seemed to have a permanent grin on his face,' he remembers. 'I was thrilled with the work Holly and her team did that day – they were magnificent. I felt pretty helpless standing around watching, but I wanted to be there for Timmy. The day worked out at the top of my expectations – it was everything I could have wished for. Even though Timmy was going to be uncomfortable at first, I knew it was only a matter of time before he'd feel the full benefit of having that awful thing removed. I went home that night with a big smile on my face too.'

The next day, Anthony took Timmy back to the animal centre, to a comfortable bed in his own kennel and run. Although he knew the old boy was now being well looked after, Anthony realized that, given he was an elderly dog, it was unlikely he would be re-homed easily. After all, he might only have a few weeks or months of life left in him. All Anthony wanted for Timmy was for his remaining life, however short, to be as comfortable as possible. It was the least he deserved.

In the course of his work on another case, Anthony had been dealing with Emma Fishbourne, a vet who teaches herd health and management at Leahurst, the University of

Liverpool's teaching hospital for Veterinary Science, where the RSPCA uses the pathology and other specialist services. The following day he contacted Emma.

'I've picked up this amazing dog, a little old collie. He's survived a long, tricky operation, but we don't know how long he's got – probably not too long – and I really want him to spend his final days in a home environment, as happy as possible, not in kennels. Do you know anyone who would take him?'

That same afternoon, Emma was having tea with a vet colleague, Jo Oultram, and Jo's husband, Thomas, who runs a dairy farm in Cheshire with his brother. Emma knew Jo and Thomas had another rescued collie cross, Max, and that they'd previously had yet another elderly collie cross, Sheba, who reached the grand old age of seventeen. She read Anthony's text to them, and within five minutes Jo and Thomas had agreed to foster Timmy.

'We thought that a nice, little old dog would be good company for my mother-in-law,' said Jo, whose in-laws also live on the farm, in a house just a few yards away from hers.

'We also knew that because of the jobs we do, on a pragmatic level we accept the loss of animals, and we weren't fazed by the fact that we might not have very long with Timmy. A lot of people wouldn't take him on – with the prospect of his life possibly being very short – but we're used to seeing the lives of animals come to an end. We thought that whatever we could give him had to be better than him spending the rest of his life in kennels, hoping to be fostered.'

Emma put Jo in touch with Anthony, who was delighted that his new canine friend might now have an unexpectedly happy final chapter to his life. He was thrilled to, in turn, be able to put Jo in touch with Kay, the kennel manager at the animal centre, who immediately invited her to come up and see Timmy.

When Jo arrived, Timmy was sitting on a blanket in the office, and her first thought was that he was the spitting image of her old dog, Sheba. 'That sold him to me. We'd decided to take him anyway, but that convinced me that he was our dog.'

Kay was happy to let Jo sign the paperwork and foster Timmy there and then. Normally, thorough checks are made on new owners to ensure they'll be able to cope with the animals they're taking on, and they're usually expected to visit the kennels a few times to make sure they've bonded with their chosen dog. Kay thought it was best for Timmy to recover somewhere he could be monitored, and the normal fostering procedure be followed until his case was heard and he could be officially re-homed.

'They knew I was a vet, that I'm used to dogs – especially this breed – and that I'd cope,' explained Jo. 'I think everyone felt that the sooner Timmy was settled in a new home, the better. If they'd wanted me to go in every day to see him for a while, I'd have done it – whatever was needed. But I came with recommendations from Emma and Anthony, and it seemed kindest to let him come to his new home as soon as possible.'

The first Anthony knew of it was a phone call from Kay: 'Timmy's gone.'

Anthony's heart sank. 'What do you mean?' he asked hurriedly, really worried. His first thought was that Timmy hadn't made it, that his age and the stress of the operation had caught up with him.

'Jo's been in and she's taken him,' Kay elaborated. 'Where better for him to recover than with a vet?'

Where better indeed. Anthony was delighted – and relieved.

Timmy had spent four days at the kennels, and had been sleeping in the reception area all day, where staff could not only make sure he didn't scratch himself and rip his stitches, but also give him lots of love and affection and try to cheer him up. He was still on considerable pain relief, and for the first couple of days he had struggled to open his mouth to eat and to yawn. However, by the time Jo took him home he was already on the road to recovery. His head was up, his tail was wagging, and he was clearly loving all the fuss he was receiving.

She remembers how he came home wearing a buster collar to prevent him scratching his face wound, but he clearly didn't like it, so she took it off. She kept an eye on whether he was bothering with his stitches, knowing she could take action if he was, being a vet herself. It made him happier to have the collar off, and he didn't scratch the wound, although her other dog Max licked it a couple of times.

Happiness was soon in full supply for Timmy and it felt like the first time he'd ever known it. He found a home on the sofa, in a spacious, comfy, clean home, and he and six-year-old Max became great friends from their first meeting. After just a couple of days Timmy was joining Jo and Max for walks through the fields and woods near the farm. If ever Timmy lags behind or wanders off, Jo gives Max the command, 'Go find Tim,' and the younger collie trots off to round up elderly Timmy, who is usually enjoying a good sniff at something. Max seems to understand instinctively that his pal can't go as fast or as far as he can, and he makes allowances for him, always happy to go at his pace . . . They're very happy trotting around the farmyard, keeping one another company.

'We can't make the whole area dog-proof — that would be impossible,' says Jo, whose husband and his brother keep

360 cows on the farm. 'But both dogs know where they're allowed to go.'

Jo herself specializes in the veterinary care of dairy cattle — she met Thomas when she came to the farm as a vet.

'I wanted to be a vet from the age of about twelve. I deviated once or twice with other ideas, but I always came back to it. I was in a mixed practice for thirteen years, but it made sense, living where I do, to specialize in farm animals.'

As well as Max and Timmy, the farm is also home to Jo's two horses and two cats, and Jo jokes that they're thinking of renaming the house The Ark. Although Max sometimes chases the cats, Tim ignores them — perhaps because of his age. Like the dogs, they've both been re-homed by Jo and Thomas.

Lucy, one of the cats, has been with the family for more than ten years, and was introduced to Jo when she was called out to treat a goat. The goat owner was fostering cats for Cats Protection, and Lucy was one of her charges. The other cat is fifteen-year-old Lucky, an elderly stray whom Jo heard about through a vet friend. When he first arrived he was very scared, hiding behind the television, but now, like the other animals, he knows he has a good home.

'We've got a good track record with the age of our animals. Sheba made it to seventeen, and she was a fast, whippy collie right up to the day she had a stroke and died. Timmy is now over seventeen years old, if the age given by his original owner is correct. That's all we have to go on, so we have to assume it's right. He's clearly quite old, but he's very active and alert. A good mix of breeds is generally very healthy, and although we can clearly see Tim is a typical black-and-tan collie, goodness knows what else is in there. He's a very tough little dog to have survived everything.'

She's never known a dog settle in so fast and thinks Max

has helped a lot, as Timmy seems to really enjoy following his new friend. Perhaps at some time in his past he lived with another dog? All that fear he showed when he was first rescued has completely gone, though. He's very accepting of things and, in Jo's words, 'he's certainly got a good enough brain'.

He lives with Jo and Thomas, but frequently visits Thomas's parents in their house near by. 'He knows he's welcome in both houses,' explains Jo. 'He also knows that if he scampers round to my mother-in-law and looks at her with pleading eyes, he'll get a biscuit. Then he'll trot back here and do the same . . . It's hilarious watching him playing people off one another for dog biscuits. He may be an old dog, but the minute he hears anyone go into the kitchen, he can hurdle the back of the sofa to get there, just in case there's a treat on offer.'

His new buddy Max had come to live with Jo and Thomas after Sheba died, when Jo put out the word that they were looking for another collie as a pet, not a working dog. A friend told them about Max, who was up for re-homing because his owners couldn't cope with an energetic collie in a small home. Max has been castrated, which can help curb the urge to wander, but Timmy hasn't had the snip, and because of his age neither the RSPCA or Jo wanted to put him through another operation.

'It could have been done at the same time as the tumour operation, but at that stage he didn't legally belong to the RSPCA. Now we all agree that he shouldn't have another anaesthetic. If he does wander — and he's shown no sign of doing so in over a year of living with us — I'll consider using hormone treatment. But I think he realizes he's rather well off here, and he's not going anywhere . . .'

Timmy came home with Jo as his foster carer, but both Jo and Thomas knew they wanted to keep him for good. For the first few months they couldn't officially adopt him because a court case was proceeding against his owner, who had refused to sign him over to the RSPCA.

'Anthony was confident he'd win the case, but he told me to make sure I didn't lose Timmy – he was evidence! There was no question of us ever losing Tim . . .'

The owner was successfully convicted of animal welfare offences. The magistrate also gave ownership of Timmy to the RSPCA. As soon as the case was finally concluded, Timmy was officially a member of the Oultram family, and Jo and Thomas have never had any problems with him. He and Max both sleep in their bedroom: Max on the couple's bed and Timmy on his own bed. When Thomas gets up early for milking, Max goes with him, and Timmy hops up into his place on the bed with Jo.

'He doesn't seem to have nightmares about his past life. In fact, he sleeps very soundly. Sometimes I have to wake him up, and then my heart is pounding as I check that he's actually breathing,' Jo says. 'He much prefers cooler weather for walking – hot weather tires him out and I keep a closer eye on him. He has a slight heart murmur – not unusual at his age – but we don't want him panting and struggling to keep up, so we keep his walks short.'

When the farm was blanketed in snow the first winter Timmy spent there, Jo had no idea whether it was the first time he had encountered it, but he wasn't bothered by it. When Jo drove him and Max to a local forest, two minutes away, for a snowy walk, Tim promptly fell through some ice into a muddy puddle.

'I took a wonderful picture of him: a happy dog having a great time in the mud and snow. I've got another picture of him and Max, both galloping towards me, tails in the air, two very contented dogs.'

Anthony visited Timmy at the farm, three months after he settled in.

'I knew he was doing well because I'd kept in touch with Jo, but I couldn't believe how fantastic he looked. His face was almost completely healed. I could see the scar, but it was barely noticeable. The main difference was in his demeanour, though. From being terrified and miserable, he was as happy as any dog can be.

'His surroundings couldn't have been any more different from where we found him. I'll never forget walking through that door and seeing him cowering amongst all that filth. I'm very glad that I filmed it, because it is really hard to describe such squalor . . . People could see for themselves just how terrible it was, and how massive his tumour was.

'Now, instead of being on his own for days on end, he has company all the time, and everyone clearly dotes on him. I was really made up to see him. I was so worried about him when I first led him out of that awful house, where he'd been left on his own in excruciating pain. To see him now, it makes my heart sing.

'His new life is magnificent, it's all the happiness he deserves, and it's definitely given him a new lease of life. We rely on people like Jo – they're such an important part of this story – especially people who are prepared to take on an elderly dog and give him a good life for his final months or years. It's hard to find words to say how pleased I am for Timmy. I'll always keep in touch with Jo – I want to know how Timmy's getting on. Even if he doesn't have much longer left of his life, his last memories will be such good ones.'

The good memories are not just Timmy's. What he has brought to Jo and Thomas's life has made it a mutually beneficial relationship that has been hugely rewarding.

Hopefully Timmy still has many months ahead of him,

but when his time comes, Jo is confident she and Thomas will make a point of asking the RSPCA if they have another elderly dog that needs a home: 'We'll definitely do it again. It's a great feeling to have given him these happy times at the end of his life, but he's also brought great fun and affection to us.'

TIPS ON HOW TO CARE FOR YOUR DOG

Older dogs

ON AVERAGE, dogs live for around twelve years, although many live for much longer. Individual animals age at different rates, but there are things owners can do to keep an older dog happy and healthy.

Regular health checks are really important for ageing animals and can mean any potential health problems are detected early. This can help prevent and manage disease, can ultimately be less costly, and helps to give pets a better quality of life. Some vets even run dedicated clinics for senior pets and their owners.

As they get older, dogs' dietary requirements change. This will vary with breed and size, but at around the age of seven they might benefit from moving on to a diet designed specifically for senior dogs. Many brands are available in pet stores, supermarkets and from veterinary practices, and should be complete and well balanced to provide the right nutrients. They also take into account the fact that older dogs may be less active and need fewer calories. Owners should seek veterinary advice before changing their dog's diet, and always make any changes gradually to avoid stomach upsets.

Although they may be slowing down, senior dogs still need regular exercise — not only does it give them the opportunity to explore and meet other dogs and people,

▶

but it's also important for preventing excessive weight gain. However, they may need shorter walks, little and often.

Slowing down somewhat with old age is normal, but if your dog seems stiff or has trouble with tasks such as getting out of bed and going upstairs, seek advice from a vet as there may be treatments that can help. Pets are often stoic and may suffer in silence, so try to be observant.

We may think that some changes in our pet's health or behaviour are just down to 'old age', such as being less playful or losing weight, but these changes may actually have a medical cause and need treatment. So it's important to be on the lookout and take your dog to the vet if you notice a change in their behaviour or think something may not be quite right.

CHAPTER 2

Clover

THE LITTLE puppy was sitting patiently outside a house in a pretty market town in the west of England. For such a quiet, attractive setting, she was an unexpectedly shocking sight. Black duct tape had been bound so tightly around her muzzle that she couldn't open her mouth to bark, eat, drink, or even pant. With blood supply restricted, her nose below the binding was grossly swollen. Watery blood dripped from the muzzle, and, once you got close enough, it was clear that the foul and distinct stench of rotting tissue was coming from her.

The whippet had been found, running distractedly through the streets, by the family who lived in the house, and they were doing their best to care for her as they waited for the RSPCA to arrive. RSPCA Inspector Nikki Denham had been an hour's drive away when the call came through, and she raced to the scene as fast as she could.

The family had put a bowl of water down for the thirsty dog, but Nikki could see the tape was wound so tightly she was unable to drink a drop. It was a hot summer's day, and Nikki knew the whippet puppy would be overheating, as the main way a dog cools itself down is by losing heat through its mouth while panting. It meant dehydration would be setting in. The situation was life-threatening.

Despite the barbaric treatment she'd endured, the dog peered up at Nikki with big, trusting eyes. First things first. Nikki quickly checked for a microchip but wasn't surprised when she didn't find one. In her experience, microchipped dogs are more likely to be cared-for and less likely to get treated like this. Nikki's first instinct was to remove the tape that was causing the puppy so much distress, but she knew better than to attempt it herself, and she was relieved that the family who found her had not tried to cut her free either: this little dog needed the careful attention of a vet who could sedate her before attempting to get it off. It wasn't going to be easy.

Lifting the puppy gently, Nikki carried her carefully to the van, settling her as comfortably as possible, and rang the nearest vet to ask if they could cope with a desperate emergency.

'They were great. They said to bring her straight in. As I drove, the van filled with the stench of decaying flesh. I had to fight back tears at the thought of anyone doing such a senseless, cruel thing to such a placid, gentle dog,' remembers

Nikki. 'If someone doesn't want a dog, they can take it to an RSPCA animal centre. Why do something so mindlessly cruel?'

Until Nikki walked in carrying her limp bundle, it had been a normal Saturday morning for vet Tanya Crawley at Vets4Pets. The practice was open for half a day, and three or four owners with their pets were in the waiting area, all with appointments to see Tanya.

When they saw Nikki's uniform and the anguish on her face, then caught the stench from the little dog's wounds, they all realized that Tanya was going to be flat out working on an animal who desperately needed her skills, and whose treatment had to take priority over the routine requirements of their well-cared-for pets.

'I am so proud of my clients,' said Tanya. 'They could see this was a huge emergency, and they all went to reception and re-booked appointments, never complaining, all aware that the dog in Nikki's arms needed help immediately. It's a day that is etched into my memory. And so it should be. Cruelty like that should never be forgotten.'

All Tanya knew before Nikki walked in was that she was bringing a dog with its muzzle taped shut. It was only when she saw the forlorn puppy, who was just seven or eight months old at the time, that she realized how serious the problem was.

'Seeing Nikki carrying her in replays in my mind, almost in slow motion. Whoever put that tape on her used real force – she must have been gripped very tightly. I'm haunted by the image of a strong man doing it to this defenceless little dog, saying "Right, you," and pinning her down, winding the tape as tight as he could. It might not have been a man, but it had to be someone strong, and someone very cruel.

'Occasionally, a bandage on a pet is too tight, and when

the area swells it has to be cut off. But this was something far, far worse – something deliberately meant to do harm.'

The shiny black tape had to come off, but the smell coming from it told Tanya that it was deeply embedded, and that the flesh around it was rotting and infected. The little dog did not struggle, even before she was given a full anaesthetic so that the tape could be removed without causing any further suffering. It was as though her pain had taken her beyond fear. She was so close to death from severe dehydration and her prolonged pain that there was very little fight left in her, so she allowed herself to be handled without any fuss.

When the tape was carefully and gently cut away, much of the puppy's skin and part of her lips at both sides came away too. Tanya cut out some of the obviously dead tissue, but she knew that more would probably have to be removed. The skin was still atrophying, and she needed to see how much of it was going to die before she cut any more away. She was desperate not to remove any that could be saved.

She also thought she might need to perform skin grafts on the dog's face, as it wasn't clear whether new skin would grow to cover such a large wound. However, at this early stage it was important simply to go slowly, and hope to preserve as much of the damaged flesh as possible and give her a fighting chance at pulling through.

When the operation was finally over, Tanya, her staff and Nikki from the RSPCA weren't confident that the whippet would survive, but Tanya knew they had given it their best shot. The little dog was started on a course of antibiotics as a matter of urgency, and given some pain relief. Now, all she needed was a name, and one of the nurses at the vet practice picked Clover, because she was lucky to have been rescued in the nick of time, and without such swift attention wouldn't have stood a chance.

'In the big scheme of things she was a very unlucky little dog, but from the moment Nikki found her, her luck changed dramatically. And, besides, Clover seemed to suit her,' says Tanya.

When the patient regained consciousness after the operation, she quickly demonstrated her will to survive, eating and drinking as soon as she was able. She was clearly starving. She hadn't been able to manage anything while the tape had bound her muzzle, which at best guess must have been a day or two – she would've died from dehydration had it been any longer. A couple of days without food or water still had potentially disastrous consequences for her health, as she was already seriously underweight. She was clearly a fighter, though, and the philosophy that rings true for anyone working with abused and neglected dogs is that you have to fight for an animal who is a fighter.

Leaving little Clover to rest and recover, Tanya finally went home, satisfied that she'd done all she could for the time being. Once home, she shared Clover's story with her husband, Dan.

'I don't normally tell Dan about all the animals I treat. I try to keep home and work separate. But I was so shaken by little Clover I told him everything. I'm resilient normally – it goes with the job. I'm not hardened – I still weep when I lose a patient, because they're someone's loved pet – but I know it's part of my job. While I was working on Clover I was able to stay detached and professional, but afterwards I felt fragile, vulnerable, a bit shaky. Even though it was a lovely summer afternoon, I lay on the sofa with a glass of wine – I hardly ever drink – and a bar of chocolate, with a blanket over me. I was really upset.'

Then something bizarre happened that made the day even more memorable. Dan called through from the kitchen, 'Tanya, there's a black cat in one of the kitchen cupboards.'

To their surprise, a flea-ridden cat — with no collar or identity tag — had taken refuge in the kitchen. After quickly checking him over, Tanya put him in the crate belonging to the family's lurcher, Pablo, another RSPCA rescue dog, with some food and water. She wondered what was going on: was there a neon sign flashing over her head, attracting sick and distressed animals?

The cat's arrival was a strange event — nothing like that had ever happened before or has happened since — and particularly odd considering there were already so many other animals in the house. You'd have thought Tanya and Dan's two dogs and own cat would have put the stray off coming in.

The next day, a Sunday, Tanya took the cat into the clinic very early for treatment, and to get the ball rolling on his re-homing. But mainly she wanted to check on Clover.

'As soon as I arrived I heard a really loud, penetrating barking noise: it was Clover, and her bark was probably why some cruel owner had decided to tape her mouth shut. It was a horrible racket. She really didn't like being in the clinic kennels.'

In some ways the noise was a healthy sign: the little dog was feeling well enough to complain about her surroundings.

As Tanya checked her over again, it was clear that Clover was going to need extensive treatment, and it was going to take some time. However, after three days the staff at the clinic told Tanya that they, and the other sick animals, were suffering because of Clover's barking, which was at a peculiar pitch that set everyone's teeth on edge. This was when Tanya decided she would take Clover home with her, on a temporary basis.

Clover wasn't the first animal to have come home with Tanya, whose children Maya, twelve at the time, and Kiran, then thirteen, had grown accustomed to sharing their home with fostered dogs, cats and rabbits from the vet practice.

'Tanya brings them all home, rather than leave them for too long living in a cage at the clinic,' explains Dan. 'We've had one-eyed dogs, dogs with no fur, a cat with brain damage. Tanya says it's perfectly normal, and that all vets do it . . . Sometimes the animals stay for a few days, some, like our lurcher Pablo, never leave us.'

At times, it's the only way to take a dog's healing to the next level.

As soon as she was away from the clinic, Clover stopped her persistent howling. She was still very poorly and, over the course of the next eight weeks, had to return briefly to the clinic for four more operations, each one under general anaesthetic, including an operation to spay her. Where the tape had been removed, her nasal bones were visible on the top of her muzzle, and there was a deep wound under her chin, as well as the damage to her mouth and teeth. She had to have poultices applied to her face for six weeks, to help remove the dead skin and tissue, and her dressings had to be changed five or six times a day to prevent further infection. Tanya showed Dan and Maya how to do it, so that Clover didn't have to go into the clinic every day.

'Dan and Maya are the unsung heroes – they did the essential work,' Tanya acknowledges modestly. 'But Clover was a star, allowing her face to be dressed all the time with saline dressings, which must have been painful, and she took her tablets with no fuss. It's as if she knew it was for her own good.'

'It didn't take long to learn how to do the dressings,' remembers Maya. 'We had to soak the bandages in a saline solution and keep changing them, about five times a day. We also had to use an antiseptic spray on her wounds. Even after everything she went through, she didn't mind us touching her. She seemed to know we were trying to help.'

Each time Tanya operated, she tried to reconstruct the little dog's face, but it was incredibly difficult with so little viable flesh. A week after the first operation to remove the tape, Tanya had to cut away more flesh that was clearly dead. She put small stitches round the gaping wound on Clover's nose, to allow bandages to be anchored. There was a moment when it looked as though Tanya would have to do a skin graft, because she couldn't see how to fix the front of Clover's nose to the rest of her face. However, luckily, after removing more dead tissue, pink flesh began to appear – living flesh. There was no concern about how Clover's face looked cosmetically, just pure delight that the wound was healing.

'Her lips were another problem, as it was impossible to reconstruct them where the tape pulled them off. They don't meet now, which makes her a bit of a sloppy eater, but it also means I've had to remove a couple of teeth. They aren't protected by her mouth closing and would rapidly decay from exposure. When she's eating you can hear a whistling noise as she sucks air in, but it doesn't affect her appetite. It didn't take too long to get her back to the right weight, and she loves her food.'

The most worrying of all the little dog's injuries was a huge hole under her chin. Tanya could see the top of her muzzle beginning to heal over her nasal bones, even though the skin was fragile and thin, but the wound underneath took much longer. All that Tanya could do was clean it daily and apply antibiotic cream, and hope that it would heal eventually. Mercifully, with each day that passed Clover continued to get stronger, and she seemed to be winning the battle to survive.

★

A few days after Clover's treatment began, RSPCA Inspector Sharon Chrisp popped in to the clinic to see her. Sharon covers the area where Clover was found, but was off duty the weekend the little dog was brought in by her colleague Nikki.

'Nikki told me about her, but I was still horrified when I saw her, even though she was apparently looking better than when she was brought in,' said Sharon. 'The swelling on her nose had gone down, but her wounds looked terrible, and even at this stage I wasn't sure she would make it. The first time I saw her at the clinic she was very vocal, so that's almost certainly the reason she was taped.'

Despite her best efforts, Sharon was unable to track down the owners responsible for Clover's appalling treatment. The police took away the tape once it had been removed from her face, to see if they could find any forensic evidence on it, but drew a blank. The RSPCA launched a press and Facebook appeal for information, and for donations to cover Clover's treatment. They raised a remarkable £14,000 from the public.

'They were clearly as horrified as we were,' admits Sharon, who has been an inspector for more than eleven years, and ranks Clover as one of the worst examples of cruelty she has ever seen. To everyone's dismay, no reliable information came in about the perpetrators, but the team fully understood that whoever had put the tape on had done it deliberately. This was not a case of neglect, but downright cruelty.

Clover settled in well at home with Tanya and Dan, but the couple were firm in the early weeks that they were only fostering her during her treatment, and that eventually she would go to an RSPCA re-homing centre. The couple already had a full house – an ancient dog called Bean, who was a rescue that Tanya and Dan had taken on when they were both at university in Liverpool, and an equally ancient black cat called Yoda, who was also adopted from the RSPCA.

'Then we had Pablo the lurcher, and he was pretty much a full-time job,' admits Dan.

Pablo had been taken in by the RSPCA when his owner went to prison, leaving him in a chaotic home with two other dogs and inadequate care. The owner's family were unable to adopt him. He and the other dogs, both terriers, were brought to Tanya by the RSPCA to be checked over before being taken to the re-homing centre. The two little terriers were confident and happy, very friendly with the staff, and would, Tanya knew, be re-homed without any problems. Pablo, on the other hand, was terrified, and it was his vulnerability that Tanya fell in love with.

Even though it was clear he had problems, Tanya decided fairly quickly that he would come to live with her family. Bean, their old mongrel, accepted him, but it took a long time for Pablo to settle in. He slept with one eye open he was so scared. He clearly didn't like men, was very afraid of them, and has remained wary to this day. He particularly doesn't take to tall men, or men with beards – which is three strikes against Tanya's husband. In the beginning, every time Dan walked into a room, Pablo would walk out.

The family had had Pablo for a year when Clover arrived to be fostered. His fearful behaviour was improving very slowly, but it was hard for Dan – who during the day was his main carer – to exercise and look after a dog who showed him no affection. Amazingly, soon after Clover walked in, there was an incredible transformation in Pablo.

'Clover has terrible physical scars and wounds, but Pablo's

scars are internal,' acknowledges Tanya. 'Clover, despite being a very poorly dog, released something in Pablo. As soon as she was strong enough, they started playing together, something Pablo had never done before. I don't think he knew what play was, and she unleashed the puppy in him.

'I have a video of them two weeks after the first operation to remove Clover's tape. She's covered in bandages, with a buster collar round her neck, and she's tearing around the garden with Pablo, digging holes and causing mayhem. It was wonderful to see them both – damaged little dogs, so very happy together. Clover is a loving soul – she loves her life and, despite what's happened to her, she loves people. She's at her happiest lying on the sofa with her family around her.'

Clover wasn't perfect, and came with some of her own behavioural problems. She hadn't been house-trained by whoever had previously owned her, and this was a big problem. Without fail, she did her business inside the house – for some reason it was as if she was afraid to do it outside. It didn't matter if Dan had taken her for a three-mile walk, she'd come home and immediately poo on the rug in the hall. Tanya or Dan would put her out in the garden, where she'd have a good sniff round, then she'd come in and squat in the house.

'I suspect she'd been kept in a confined space, perhaps a kennel with a run,' says Dan, 'and she was used to doing it on her own territory because she wasn't taken out. So she associated having a poo with being in familiar surroundings at home. It took a while to train her out of it.'

Nor did she like being left alone, even with the other dogs, which was another difficulty for the family. At night she was only happy if she was left to sleep on the sofa, but Tanya and Dan couldn't allow her to do that because she still wasn't properly toilet trained. All this meant it took some time for her to settle, and the investment in her made by Tanya and Dan was considerable.

Tanya and Dan had only originally intended to foster Clover until she was physically well enough to be re-homed. She'd been with them for around eight weeks by this point, and the day that Sharon was due to take her to the re-homing centre was fast approaching.

'I knew I would be willing to have her,' remembers Tanya. 'And so would Maya – she loves all the animals I bring home. Kiran helps with them, but he's not as fond of them as Maya. Most of all it had to be a decision that involved Dan, because I work long hours and the everyday care of the dogs devolves to him. Also, it would be very easy for me to adopt lots of the animals I treat. I see many dogs and cats that need re-homing and it's tempting to take them all on, but it always has to be a family decision.

'I'm aware that other people who work in my profession – or who work with animals in any way – may accuse me of anthropomorphizing, but I really believe there's a deep connection between an injured or neglected animal and the person who rescues them. I've seen the RSPCA films of dogs meeting the inspector who first rescued them, months later, and there's a real recognition, a real feeling of affection and kinship.

'It was Nikki who rescued Clover, but I was there from the beginning and all the way through her long treatment, and I feel a real bond with her. She was a broken being when she came to the clinic, and she put her head in our laps so gently, as if to say, "Please help me." I almost feel she chose us. She's a very special little dog.'

For Dan, being really sure that he wanted to add Clover to the family on a full-time basis was a decision that went right up to the wire. He could see why Tanya and Maya wanted to keep her, but knew that it would be him who would end up doing the lion's share of her care. The thing was, while Pablo hated him on sight, Clover gave him affection, in the same way that Bean did from the very start, and that's how she wormed her way into his heart and their lives.

On her supposed last day with the family, when Clover was physically recovered enough to move on to the RSPCA re-homing centre and Sharon was coming to pick her up, Tanya and Dan walked Clover around the small town where they live. Dan was trying to be pragmatic, knowing that because she was such a young dog they would be taking on a long-term commitment – possibly for another fifteen years. The couple called in at the post office on their walk.

Dan explained: 'We told Debbie, who works there, that we couldn't keep her and she said, "How sad for little Clover." I think that was when emotion took over, and I started to see that the pluses outweighed the minuses. On the plus side, she got on so well with Pablo, who wasn't the easiest dog to live with, and she loved us all, including me. On the minus side, there was the long, uphill struggle with toilet training, and she didn't know how to behave with other dogs she met when we were out. She would get so excited, become very noisy and turn every encounter into a big kerfuffle.'

In the end, he decided the scales were tipped in Clover's favour. The lucky little thing would be staying with them permanently.

Tanya quickly rang Sharon, who was all set to take Clover to the re-homing centre later that day, to give her the good news.

'I felt such relief that Tanya and Dan were going to keep her,' recalls Sharon. 'I knew how well they would look after her, and with all her injuries I was so pleased she'd be with the vet who understood everything about her.'

Today Clover still carries the obvious signs of her terrible abuse. The skin on her nose is very thin and pink – and has to be protected with sun cream even in the winter – and her wounds still weep. Her lips will never look normal – though her mouth is working well enough for her to eat and drink well. Physically, she'll never be the dog she once was. A skin graft on her nose would improve her appearance, but Tanya questions what the point would be. Clover is very happy and healthy. She doesn't care how she looks, and neither does her new family. The professional view is: why put her through more surgery?

Meanwhile, Dan has been working with an animal behaviourist to get on top of Clover's social problems when she meets other dogs. He explained how she missed out on all the natural socializing she should have done as a puppy, meaning it's been a long, slow process to help her get used to other dogs.

'We're getting there . . .' Dan smiles. 'With the help of lots of treats.'

The family also has to be careful when she's out and off the lead, as she'll eat anything she comes across and thinks is edible.

In Tanya's words, she's 'a real pickle'. She's a very kind-hearted dog, according to the vet, and that's her main character trait. 'When she first came into the practice, she was timid and forlorn. But her real personality is that she's a very giving, fun-loving, "I love everyone" kind of dog. That's the true Clover. She only ever made that high-pitched bark when she was in kennels, and I suspect she was kept caged for much of her early life.

'Now she's perfectly normal, apart from her disfigurement.

You can't always treat her as a special case, though — she needs training and guidance like any dog, and she's had to learn right from wrong and know the boundaries. We don't make excuses for her behaviour now.'

Strangers tend to stare, and the first question asked is about Clover's nose. Seeing it for the first time, people assume it's a fresh wound because the skin still looks so pink and fragile, but most local people now know her and are aware of her inspirational story. 'I don't mind repeating it when people ask, and then you frequently find they have a rescue story to tell you, too,' says Dan.

The great bonus of Clover's arrival for the Crawley family is the transformative effect she has had on Pablo, almost from the moment they met. The two dogs are as thick as thieves now, and Clover has helped him become a much more confident, friendly dog. Both are still frightened at night, and hate being walked after dark, so they sleep together in the family's sunroom. Bean, their old companion, who took no notice of her younger housemates, has since died, as has the family's old cat, so the whippet and the lurcher now have the place to themselves.

Back to full strength, Clover is full-on from the moment she wakes up.

'As soon as we come downstairs she's leaping about. Everything is black and white, on or off for Clover. The minute we're up, she's bouncing around at a hundred miles an hour, demanding to be taken for a walk. She doesn't understand you might like a cup of tea before you go out,' says Dan.

Tanya and Dan both had dogs when they were children, and they understand the value of pets to children. Dan's parents adopted a stray whippet when he was about five or six, and his parents have kept the same breed ever since. As a result, he's always been confident around dogs. 'I've definitely gone up in my parents' estimation since we took in a lurcher and a whippet,' he admits.

Despite not having a dog at the time, by the age of five Tanya was clear in her mind that she was going to be a vet when she grew up. When she had the opportunity to do work experience at school, it was to rule out other jobs, not to rule them in.

By then there was a family dog, acquired when she was nine or ten.

'Mum was horrified when Dad and I came back from Battersea Dogs Home with a sandy-coloured mongrel who was part German shepherd, part Labrador — maybe some other breeds in there. We didn't know anything about looking after dogs, and that wasn't just our family, it was normal at the time. We've learnt so much more in the last thirty years about caring for domestic animals. But our first dog, Lucy, was a lovely, loving dog, who quickly became part of our family.

'My mother died when I was sixteen, and then Lucy died when I was in my second year at university. It was only then that I realized what a crutch she'd been to the whole family when Mum passed away — holding me, my sister and my dad together as we grieved. Mum was different for all of us, and Lucy seemed to sense what each of us needed.

'The bond between humans and animals is something I feel passionately about, and am fascinated by. Pets are particularly beneficial for children: it doesn't matter what's been happening in their world, even if they're in trouble for not doing homework or not clearing up their room, the dog loves them unconditionally, and they can share their secrets. It's a really powerful thing.'

While her son, Kiran, is happy to walk and feed the dogs, the deep natural affinity Tanya feels with animals is also shared by her daughter, Maya. It's Maya who regularly snuggles up with Pablo and Clover; who struggles to watch animals suffer and feels strongly about the injustice of cruelty to them. However, seeing what the job of being a vet involves seems to have put her off following her mother into veterinary practice. She has no desire to watch animals in pain; her pleasure would come from meeting lots of dogs and, if possible, avoiding what she calls the 'gory bits'. The least enjoyable task, she says, would be informing owners that their beloved pets are dying.

Tanya's exceptional abilities as a vet were recognized in 2017 when she was runner-up in a nationwide competition run by a pet insurance company to find the Vet of the Year – a humbling experience that so many people voted for her and a great accolade for the often unsung work that she does. Although Tanya doesn't think the nomination was necessarily anything to do with her treatment of Clover, both the RSPCA inspectors involved with Clover's case – Nikki, who found her, and Sharon, who followed up with her – are grateful to Tanya for the emergency work she did that day as a vet, and for then taking on Clover as a member of her own family. She saved her life.

'On the day I brought Clover in, Tanya went way beyond the call of duty, clearing everything else from her diary to treat a desperately needy little dog. It's wonderful how she and her family have transformed that very depressed, subdued little animal into a cheeky, carefree dog, which is obviously her true personality,' says Nikki.

'Seeing happy, healthy animals is why we do what we do, and gets us through the horrors that we see. It's just a shame there's no justice for the offenders who inflicted this horrendous injury on a defenceless little puppy.

'I do this work because I love animals and I hate cruelty. In this job we can improve animal welfare, if only on a case-by-case basis. But all the cases add up. It's really great to be able to seek justice for abused animals. Stories like Clover's make it all worthwhile.'

TIPS ON HOW TO CARE FOR YOUR DOG

Barking

DOGS BARK for many different reasons. They may bark to express how they're feeling — for example, when they're excited, frustrated, bored or scared. If a dog feels threatened they might bark to tell somebody to stay, or go away. Sometimes dogs bark because they want something, such as their favourite toy. Dogs may also bark when they're in distress — if they're left alone, for instance.

Barking is a form of communication and is a normal behaviour. However, if the amount a dog barks increases, or becomes excessive, it can be a sign that something isn't right. It might also be causing problems for neighbours and other dog walkers if the dog barks while being walked.

If this happens, it's important to address any underlying problems that could be causing the dog to bark more. Because dogs bark for so many different reasons it can be difficult to understand exactly what the cause is. Is your dog getting enough exercise? For most dogs, just having access to the garden isn't enough — they need opportunities every day to burn off energy through walks and play time.

If your dog is barking unduly or more than usual, it's always best to speak to your vet. There may be an undiagnosed health issue — problems with your dog's ears or hearing could be causing the barking, for example. Your vet may also refer you to a trainer or behaviour expert

▶

for further help; these specialists will be able to identify why your dog is barking and work with you to develop a tailored treatment plan.

It's also really important never to punish unwanted behaviour as it could cause fear and pain, and make the problem worse.

CHAPTER 3

Lily (aka Snoopy)

L ILY CAME into the lives of John and Hazel Catt on a bitterly cold winter's evening. They were driving Hazel's sister Maureen home. It was 7.15 p.m. and had already been dark for several hours. As they rounded a bend, the car's headlights picked out something in the road, close to the kerb, that looked like an abandoned bundle of rags. Traffic was swerving around it, but John was concerned the obstruction might cause an accident. He decided to pull over. He got out of the car, thinking the pile was just some rubbish, but as he walked towards it, he could see that it was moving.

A small head rose from the bundle.

'It's a little dog,' John shouted back to Hazel and Maureen, who then both got out of the car to take a closer look.

At first, John assumed the dog had been hit by a car, but after quickly checking her over he could find no injuries – although it was clear she was painfully thin and extremely cold, and didn't even have the strength to get to her feet. She was wearing a dirty, wet, red dog coat.

'I ran my hand over her back to see if there were any problems, and it was awful. There was no meat on her at all. I could feel every bone, and her neck was like a little tube,' remembers John.

He found an old blanket in the boot of his car, and carefully wrapped it around the emaciated lurcher. Just her tiny head and big, glassy, frightened eyes peeped through. He carried her as they made their way down the road, knocking on nearby doors to see if anybody knew where she had come from. Nobody had any idea; no one recognized her. She wasn't a local dog, they were told.

John, Hazel and Maureen decided that it would be best to take her to the nearest emergency vet and a passer-by, out walking his own dog, told them there was a practice only five minutes away, which was still open for evening surgery.

Maureen cradled the pathetic bundle while John drove them there. Even through the blanket she could feel how cold the dog was.

They handed the sad little lurcher over, and gave their details to the receptionist. That should have been the end of their Good Samaritan deed – they had scooped up an animal in trouble and put her into safe hands – but none of them could get the little dog out of their mind, so shocked had they been by her condition.

'We couldn't work out how she'd become so skeletal,' said John. 'If someone had deliberately starved her, it just didn't bear thinking about.'

That night, both Hazel and Maureen slept badly, waking constantly to think about their find. As soon as the vet's opened the next morning, Maureen called in to ask how the skinny stray had got on overnight. She was delighted to hear that the lurcher had survived, but only just. Her organs had been shutting down through starvation and she'd been suffering from hypothermia. Maureen was told 'she's hanging on', so was clearly still in grave danger and not yet out of the woods. She was quick to phone Hazel with the news.

'It was such a relief,' recalls Hazel. 'We really weren't sure she'd pull through even one night. I said to Maureen, "I've been thinking of names for her," and Maureen said, "So have I." Amazingly, we both thought of "Lily". Just a coincidence, but looking back it seemed like fate. I told John and he said, "Lily it is, then." That's when I thought, "Ooh, looks like we're having her . . ."'

Until that point, John and Hazel had absolutely no intention of ever having another dog. Their beloved boxer, Ricky, had died eight years earlier, the third in a line of beautiful dogs who had shared their home. The grief of losing Ricky made Hazel feel that she couldn't go through the loss of a pet again; instead, they were content enough looking after their daughter's dog from time to time.

However, Lily had stirred a deep love in them, even after just a short meeting. Something about her sad state had touched them deeply. They understood that her life still hung in the balance, but they decided there and then that, if she regained her health, they would offer to adopt her.

RSPCA Inspector Rosie Russon first heard about the emaciated little stray the morning after her rescue, when the vet practice called her. Even though Rosie had eighteen years' experience behind her, she was shocked by the sight that greeted her when she reached the practice.

'She was the thinnest dog I have ever seen that was still alive. Dogs whose body weight has sunk so low don't normally survive. I think she was within a couple of hours of death when John, Hazel and Maureen picked her up from the road. They saved her life. So many other cars, probably full of busy commuters, had been swerving round her and ignoring the bundle, so she was extremely lucky that John pulled over. I couldn't believe the sight of her – she looked like a skeleton of a dog. She was heartbreakingly thin.'

The staff at the vet's had given her fluids and small portions of food, which is important with a starving animal so as not to shock their digestive system, and they had warmed her up with the help of a heat mat. They'd washed her red coat, and she was wearing it again when Rosie first met her. By that time she could stand up for a few seconds, which she hadn't been able to do the night before, but she collapsed again very quickly.

'She was a pitiful little thing; very quiet, very timid,' Rosie remembers with sadness. 'She allowed me to take photographs of her terrible condition without moving – it's usually a tricky job because dogs bounce around.'

The lurcher weighed just 10kg, when her minimum weight should have been 18–25kg. There were small wounds on her head and body, pressure sores from where she had been lying, because there was absolutely no fat to cushion her and she probably hadn't had comfortable bedding.

The tip of her tail had broken off and the bone was exposed, which is a typical injury for dogs like lurchers when they've been kept in an enclosed space, such as a kennel or a run, for a long time. It isn't a big problem medically speaking, but it would've caused her pain. The tail was later trimmed and stitched back together to ease her discomfort.

The greatest fear was that some of her internal organs – her liver, kidneys and heart – had suffered serious damage because of the dire lack of nutrition, and that they might be shutting down. She was a very lucky dog, however: all the tests to determine organ function came back clear. Recovery appeared to be just a matter of getting some fluids and food into her, and helping her regain her strength gradually.

'Even so, when I first picked her up,' said Rosie, 'I really didn't think she would survive. She'd made it through that first crucial night, but that was no guarantee, and I knew it wouldn't be plain sailing.' Sadly, starvation and dehydration can still lead to organ failure, even after the initial recovery starts.

Having no idea about the name Lily that Hazel and Maureen had come up with, Rosie also gave the little lurcher a name: Snoopy. She took her to the RSPCA animal centre at Leybourne, Kent, where the staff kept up the regime of very small meals throughout the day, and lots of fluids.

'She was a gannet, desperate for food,' Rosie recalls with fondness. 'She'd pin her bowl to the floor with one foot and lick it out. But the staff had to resist the temptation to give her more, as her digestive system, which had been compromised by her enforced starvation, had to be allowed to recover slowly.'

Rosie had grown up wanting to work with animals, but her other early ambition had been to be a police officer. When she was seventeen she joined the Royal Air Force and served in the RAF Police for nine years.

'We were RAF training in Shropshire back in the autumn of 1998 when we came across a badger that had been hit by a car, was badly injured and clearly in pain. Although we carried firearms we weren't allowed to put it out of its misery, so we called the RSPCA and the inspector was able to assess the animal and put it to sleep humanely.

'That was when I first thought about working for the

RSPCA. It's the perfect combination for me: looking after animals and also doing detective work in cases of animal cruelty. If you ask me what job I would rather do, the answer is that there isn't one.'

Rosie rang John and Hazel the day after they had handed the lurcher in, and took down the exact details of where and when they had found her. She then followed the usual procedures: she appealed for information through the press, and worked with the local police to try to identify the dog's owner.

Although there were a couple of leads, nothing could be proven, and the only explanation as to why the dog was found at the side of the road was that she had been dumped there. She was clearly too weak to have got there by herself. Whoever left her possibly hoped she'd be run over, and then her awful condition might never have been discovered. Despite her best efforts, Rosie was unable to find out who was responsible for the appalling cruelty of starving such a small dog. Now all she could do was put her trust in the staff at the animal centre, who did everything possible to help Snoopy recover.

Rosie visited Snoopy at the animal centre several times over the next few weeks, as the staff there built her strength up. She wasn't her most regular visitor, though: John and Hazel were going every day that the centre was open to see their little 'Lily'.

In the very first phone call from Rosie, the day after they had found her, the couple made their intentions clear, telling Rosie that if Lily pulled through, then they would like to give her a home. Rosie advised them to think it over for a day or two, but Hazel was already determined.

'She's coming home with us,' she told Rosie. 'As much as

we said we wouldn't have another dog, the way she's come to us is very special. I think she's meant for us.'

Hazel could see why the inspector didn't want them to rush into a commitment: at that point, it was very apparent to everyone that Lily's life was still hanging by a thread. Hazel and John knew the score. They understood that it was still touch-and-go that first weekend, but hoped more than anything that little Lily would make it.

The couple's dogs have always been a big part of their life together. As well as having three dogs of their own over the years, for eighteen months the Catts had cared for a dog belonging to Maureen's grandson. They'd also looked after their daughter Jennifer's old dog, and Jennifer now has a deaf Boston terrier, Ace, who is in training to be a 'pets as therapy' dog. He understands sign language commands, which John and Hazel have even gone to the trouble of learning for whenever they look after him.

'We've always been comfortable around dogs, and a home feels right when there's a dog in it,' says John, who was able to take their first dog, a boxer-Labrador-collie cross to work every day, on the fruit farm where he was employed. 'He'd spend the entire day there. I couldn't get out of the door without him in the morning.'

It was John and Hazel's forty-fifth wedding anniversary when they made their first trip to RSPCA Leybourne Animal Centre to enquire about Lily's condition. They were thrilled when the staff asked if they would like to see her, but when she was led out to meet them, Hazel felt her heart breaking at the sight. Lily looked skeletal. Her eyes were empty, with a vague, unfocused look to them.

When she arrived at Leybourne Animal Centre, Lily was still terrified of everything around her and was reluctant to leave the kennel block. As she neared the door she would skid to a halt, simply refusing to go any further. The care team would try two or three times to coax her out, but in the end she had to be carried.

She was still so bony when Hazel saw her, that although she wanted to stroke her, she was frightened to touch her in case it caused her further pain. She was visibly shivering, even though she was wearing her little red fleece coat. Hazel and John were told she was probably about two years old and that she was called Snoopy, a name they didn't think suited her as much as Lily, so they agreed that if she did eventually come home with them, she would definitely be Lily.

Simon McArdle, an animal care assistant at the Leybourne centre, was making sure that Lily built up her strength slowly, eating with care and gaining weight steadily. Her food was a mix of wet and dry dog food, but entirely bland, nothing to upset her very sensitive stomach, and she was given four small meals a day.

'She needed to rebuild her wasted muscles, so we gave her short intervals of time off her lead, exploring the great outdoors,' he explained. 'We made sure she didn't get too tired, but it was important that she became active. With the other dogs in the kennels, we give them one long walk every day. But with Lily, she was clearly completely exhausted through starvation, so we took her out three or four times a day for very short spells. As well as helping build her muscles again, it allowed her to interact with people and other dogs. She was reluctant to walk at first, mainly because she was so weak, so we carried her out and then put her down to potter about. Gradually she began to be happier about walking, and as her weight slowly built up, so did her muscles.'

Seven weeks after her rescue, following much hard work from Simon and the rest of the staff at the centre to help her conquer her fears, and to socialize her with other dogs, Lily was ready to go home with John and Hazel. By this time, she weighed a healthy 25kg, a good weight for a lurcher her size, and more than double the 10kg she'd weighed when they picked her up off the road.

During their visits, Lily really got to know the couple well, and was always excited to see them. They'd take her for walks around the centre grounds, and they even brought their two grandsons along to see how she got on with them. She took to them within minutes.

'She was as good as gold with them, so we were sure she'd be happy to come home with us. Now she goes silly whenever the boys visit,' says Hazel.

For the first few weeks at home with the Catts, Lily was still on four meals a day, which was later reduced to three, and she's now on just two. She had never been toilet trained – as is so often the way with neglected dogs – but she picked it up very quickly.

'She's a smart little thing; she learns fast. She'd had nothing in her life before, as far as we can tell. She'd never had a puppyhood, so she reverted to being a puppy for a while at first, which we were told might happen. She's come a long way,' says John with obvious pride. 'She's a real lurcher these days. Her face has changed completely now she has muscle and flesh round it. She still has her battle scars: you can see where she had small wounds on her face and her back, but they've healed nicely and don't bother her.'

For the first few nights after she started living with them, John and Hazel both slept downstairs to be near her, and to help her get used to being in their home. Then, John went upstairs to bed, and Hazel moved to sleeping in a chair in another room, adjacent to the sunroom where Lily's bed is, moving further away from her each night.

'She slowly got used to being on her own all night, and

though we put puppy pads down, she never messed in the night, and never whined or barked.'

Now she enjoys sleeping on a comfortable bed or on her favourite chair. She's still a timid dog, but she's gaining confidence daily, thanks to the patience and tender care of John and Hazel.

'I once shouted at her when she did something wrong,' admits John, 'and she looked absolutely terrified. She'd clearly been shouted at before. I've never raised my voice since – we've trained her entirely with treats and rewards.'

She didn't understand how to play when they first met her at the animal centre – she'd obviously never had someone take the time to have fun with her, to get down on her level and roughhouse a little. She certainly hadn't been bought any gifts either – but now she loves her toys, especially her stuffed gorilla, which Hazel has had to stitch back together a few times because Lily loves throwing it about a little too much.

However, despite her growing confidence, she remains wary of strangers who come to the house. Thankfully, it doesn't take her long to get used to new faces. She's learning to trust again.

Hazel is delighted with how Lily has settled into the family: 'She adores Maureen and our other sister, Daphne – she's all over them when they come. The first time my friend Rose came round, she hid in the kitchen, but now she's brilliant with her. It's a matter of leaving her alone and letting her calm down. She used to shake – a juddery sort of movement – when she was frightened, but she doesn't do it any more.'

A year down the line and it's still necessary to exercise Lily on a long, extendable lead, because she's not yet learned a completely reliable recall command. 'We're getting there, but we're terrified that she won't come back and may run on a road.' For John and Hazel, Lily's complete freedom is something to aim for and she's making good progress. It's Lily who recognizes when John puts on his coat to take her out, and she's at his side. It's hard to remember that at first she was scared to go outside at all.

Living in the Kent countryside, the Catts are surrounded by beautiful walks. Lily is very sure-footed, and will run straight up a very steep bank, excited by the terrain and the challenge. Although she's very happy out in the fields and woods with them, John and Hazel are also gradually getting her used to walking on pavements through their village, with people passing by.

'She wasn't very happy the first time she did it, but she kept going. She's still timid, frightened of new things, but she's getting better,' says Hazel.

Strangers in close proximity are still problematic: she cowers behind John and tries to keep as far away as possible. She's not keen on other dogs, either, but is happy enough to walk past them if they're under control on leads. The problem arises when a dog is loose, without a lead. That makes her incredibly nervous. She also becomes terrified if a dog comes up behind her. However, every time she's taken out, with patience and lots of treats she gets a little bit more settled about things that happen in the wider world beyond John and Hazel's garden, and despite the demons she sometimes has to face, her walks remain her favourite part of the day.

Like many people who re-home dogs that have had a terrible start in life, John and Hazel feel that not only is the animal lucky to have found them, but they are equally fortunate to have found their new pet, without whom their lives simply wouldn't feel complete.

As for Rosie, the RSPCA inspector, she is delighted that Lily has such a happy future.

'She has a complete bond with her new owners – she adores them and they clearly adore her. They're bringing her out of her timid shell slowly and carefully. She had a really bad start in life, and she was very lucky to survive. She deserves the best of lives, and that's what she's now got.'

Simon, who organized her gradual rehabilitation at the animal centre, is always pleased to see Lily when John and Hazel take her for a visit.

'Working in an RSPCA centre we see some sad sights, but Lily was skeletal, nothing but skin and bone. Now when I see her she's got the powerful back legs of a lurcher. She was very quiet and withdrawn at first, but now she's much livelier and happier. It's a pleasure to see the difference in her. She looks like the dog she was always meant to be.'

TIPS ON HOW TO CARE FOR YOUR DOG

Diet and nutrition

ALL DOGS and puppies need constant access to clean, fresh water and a balanced diet to keep them happy and healthy. This means a diet that is right for their age, breed/type, health and lifestyle. Adult dogs should be fed at least one nutritious meal per day.

They also need the right amount of food to make sure that they don't become over- or underweight. If they're not fed enough good-quality food they can lose weight, which can then cause health problems. Equally, being fed too much food can also cause issues. Obesity can lead to diseases such as diabetes. Owners should be guided by the instructions on their dog's food packaging, but also use common sense to adjust how much their dog needs to be fed in order to make sure they stay at a healthy weight.

There are three simple steps all owners can easily follow to check if their dog is the right weight:

1. You should be able to see and feel the outline of your pet's ribs without excess fat covering.
2. You should be able to see and feel your pet's waist and it should be clearly visible when viewed from above.
3. Your pet's belly should be tucked up when viewed from the side.

▶

If a dog doesn't pass any of these three checks, or if the owner isn't sure, then a vet or veterinary nurse can help. Equally, if an owner notices any changes in their dog's eating or drinking behaviour, it's important to seek veterinary advice.

Many human foods are dangerous for animals, such as onions, raisins and chocolate. Onions, as well as garlic, leeks, shallots and chives, can cause toxicity, even when cooked. Initially they can cause vomiting and diarrhoea in dogs, but the main effect is damage to red blood cells, resulting in anaemia. Even a small quantity of grapes or their dried products (currants, sultanas and raisins) can cause severe kidney failure in dogs, and chocolate contains a powerful stimulant called theobromine, which is similar to caffeine.

Dogs need very specific diets to meet their nutritional needs, so it's best to avoid feeding them the food we eat and only use food and treats designed specifically for them.

CHAPTER 4

Flint

As RSPCA Inspector Anthony Joynes climbed the gate into the playing field, he could already see the corpse of a fully grown badger, its prone body covered with multiple wounds, its fur plastered to its flanks with congealed blood. Extending across a wide area, the field was smeared with large patches of drying blood, darkening the grass where it had pooled. It was immediately clear to Anthony that the field, adjacent to a school in Flint, North Wales, had been used for badger-baiting – a grisly, cruel 'hobby' banned back in 1835, but which is still pursued illegally and widely (but not always) under the cover of darkness today.

Badger-baiting is a form of animal blood sport in which badgers are pitted against dogs. A baiting session typically results in the death of the badger, and possibly serious injuries, or even death, to the dogs.

Anthony crossed the field carefully, having been briefed by the man who had made the phone call to the RSPCA that there was also a large and potentially dangerous dog roaming free. From experience, Anthony knew the dogs used for fighting badgers are typically terriers and lurchers crossed with bull breeds – large, powerful dogs with great speed, trained from a young age to fight other animals. The criminals who engage in the 'sport' start the dogs off with smaller animals. They then teach the dogs to fight to the death. As the dogs get older, bigger and stronger, they'll graduate to fighting larger animals, deer and badgers. Anthony was confident that this was exactly how this badger had met its rather desperate end.

To catch badgers, the self-styled 'dog men' use terriers wearing radio locators attached to their collars. They thrust the terrier into a badger sett and the signal from the locator will tell them when the terrier has encountered the badger, and the fight is on. The men will then dig down to retrieve the dog, before encouraging the fight to continue above ground, sometimes with the larger dogs too. Eventually either the dogs will kill the badger or the 'dog men' will step in, bashing the badger over the head with a spade, or even shooting it to maim it, so they can keep their dog to fight another day. Sometimes the terriers are so badly mauled that they don't survive, but to the men, their job is done.

'The big dogs are brought out,' explains Anthony, 'to fight to the death with the badger. It's not always the badger who dies. They're very robust mammals; they don't give in.'

Anthony knew that the large dog he was searching for

now was likely to be badly injured, as the badger's wounds showed the fight had been fierce and bloody. However, experience also told him the dog would probably not be a threat to him. He treats all dogs, large or small, with some initial caution, but he's found that dogs such as the one at large, having been reared in a barbaric way, can respond incredibly well to small kindnesses and any compassion shown to them. It's likely that they've never experienced affection, never been stroked for pleasure. The public should be cautious in their presence, but Anthony wasn't too worried.

Crossing the brow of a slope in the field, he caught sight of the dog in the dip beyond, close to the back-garden fences of nearby houses. The large, black, bull mastiff-lurcher cross didn't move towards him but watched warily, one foot lifted in pain, and wagged his savagely wounded tail.

'OK, mate, OK. What have you been up to?' Anthony said calmly, as he approached. 'Bless you, you're still friendly, even though you must be in pain,' he sympathized, his voice catching as he put a slip lead on the dog and inspected his injuries.

The animal's face was a mess, puncture wounds all over it, and his nose was ripped to shreds. Deep bite wounds covered the rest of his body. Blood trickled down his swollen legs and it looked as if his jaw was badly injured and swollen too. What had happened to him was clearly not an accident.

As a display of friendship, Anthony gave the dog a tray of wet dog food, which was easy for the animal to eat despite his injuries. It's something inspectors always carry as a bargaining chip.

'I know that at some houses I visit, in my RSPCA uniform, the dog may instantly form a bad impression of me because I look like a policeman. If police have visited before, it was probably a negative interaction with the dog's owners. A dog treat or two breaks down barriers,' he explains.

In the field, the dog wolfed down the food. Anthony could see that, although he was a huge dog, he was clearly underweight. Speaking to him gently, Anthony led the injured animal slowly across the field back to the gate. Every movement caused the dog further distress as he limped along on his excruciatingly painful legs.

'OK, mate, we're going to get you some help,' Anthony reassured him. Even though the dog didn't understand, the stream of comforting words — delivered in a low, calm voice — made him raise his head and struggle again to wag his broken tail.

It was early on a Sunday morning: the call had come through at 6.45 a.m. North Wales is outside Anthony's regular patch of the Wirral and Chester, but he was covering it for the weekend. Without hesitation he had jumped out of bed, thrown on his uniform, and driven the 20 miles from his home on the Wirral to the site in Flint where the badger and dog had been spotted.

'I'd have happily driven there at two a.m. or three a.m. if I thought I had a chance of catching the men who commit these atrocities. I knew that by the time I was called there would be little chance of the culprits still being around.'

When Anthony and the injured dog arrived at the gate, a police car was already there to meet them, and someone summoned the school caretaker to open the gate. The injured dog was far too big to be lifted over it, and with his wounds it would have been desperately painful for him. While they were waiting for the caretaker to arrive, Anthony gave the dog some more food, and again he wolfed it down. He'd clearly been out all night, and was starving and dehydrated as well as in great pain. In the few moments they waited together, Anthony crouched down and stroked any bits of flesh and fur that weren't wounded, and the two cemented their friendship.

The local resident who had called the RSPCA was terribly shaken by what he saw. He felt terrible because he'd heard a scream in the night, a cry like an animal in pain. He wished he'd done something there and then, but it would've been unwise to approach the men who take part in badger-baiting and other vicious so-called sports. They're usually involved in other criminal activity, sometimes drugs or firearms, and wouldn't stop short of violence towards anyone who discovered them. RSPCA inspectors are trained in conflict management — from their initial induction to mandatory refresher courses every three years — so the man had been wise to stay away. Nonetheless, he couldn't help but reflect on what might have been if he'd acted sooner.

Anthony believes the men were probably disturbed in their 'sport', because they wouldn't normally leave a dog behind as evidence of their activities. He suspects they were spooked, perhaps by another resident calling out, or by someone approaching with a torch to investigate the unexpected noise.

'From his condition,' speculates Anthony, 'I guessed this dog was at the end of his fighting life, and I don't think he would've survived another big night of fighting. But they'd clearly been using him as a primary dog, so normally they would use him as a stud, to father other fighting dogs. If they'd decided he wasn't good enough to breed from, they would've just killed him, because to these callous criminals he wouldn't be worth the food bill.'

Being abandoned and left for dead was a lucky break for Flint, the name Anthony chose for the dog because of where he'd been found. It offered him the chance to be rescued from an unthinkable existence, although at this stage, Anthony wasn't sure he would survive his injuries.

After loading him into the van, Anthony drove Flint to the ChesterGates Referral Hospital in Chester, which was only a few miles away and is open twenty-four hours a day for urgent cases. The hospital has specialist vets available for all types of emergencies. Struggling to walk from the car park to the waiting room used the last of Flint's strength, and he collapsed on the floor, unable to go on. Anthony handed him over to the vet on duty, who put him on a drip immediately, gave him powerful antibiotics and pain relief, and settled him on a comfortable bed.

By the time Anthony collected Flint the following day, he was amazed to see that some of the superficial wounds were already scabbing over and starting to heal. With the initial emergency treatment over, he transferred Flint to the RSPCA Wirral & Chester Branch in Wallasey, where local vet Holly Jones came to check him over. In addition to his new injuries, she could see plenty of other scars and old wounds, presumably from previous fights, including a torn ear.

Holly was used to Anthony bringing her distressed and damaged animals, yet it was horrible for her to think of what Flint had been through, and to imagine what he'd been subjected to in the past. It was clear to Holly that Flint had previously suffered wounds even worse than those he was presenting with now.

She agreed with Anthony's suspicions: that Flint looked like a bull mastiff–lurcher cross, commonly known as a bull lurcher (although this is not a recognized breed, and the term also includes other lurcher types, such as Staffies crossed with greyhounds).

Flint's lips were very distended, and one of his teeth was freshly broken, with the root still in place. It was clearly causing him anguish. There were scabs all around his eyes, his nose was swollen and oozing. Callouses on his elbows showed that he was used to lying on a hard floor with no soft bedding. The good news was that, despite his sorry appearance, Holly felt that Flint's prognosis was good.

'His wounds will heal, but it will take a lot of loving care from the staff here,' she warned.

In the following weeks, Flint had two operations on his tail, which eventually had to be made much shorter. The infection from his wounds migrated into his bones, which called for even stronger antibiotics, and six teeth had to be removed. He'd already lost quite a few: out of forty-two, he now only had twenty.

Anthony managed to visit Flint most days at the animal centre, where the staff discovered their patient was, in fact, a gentle, loveable giant. They kept his bed in the reception area, so that he wasn't cooped up in a crate, but also because he was such affectionate company. Anthony would take him into the office while he dealt with paperwork, and Flint would sit with his huge head resting on Anthony's knee, his flank pressed up against his rescuer's legs. He would enjoy all the petting and comfort that came his way, as though he'd never experienced anything like it before.

For the first few weeks at the centre, his recovery was slow, and at times he looked like a completely broken dog. Someone who met him commented that he looked lost, and that his eyes were ghostlike, almost as if part of him had given up. As his pain receded and his wounds closed, he regained a light in his eyes, as if he accepted that the people who were now looking after him really cared about him, and wanted nothing more but for him to recover and be happy.

Flint's food intake was carefully monitored, bringing his

skeletal frame slowly and safely up from under 40kg to a solid 48, and once he looked healthy, vet Holly was able to estimate his age at around five or six years old.

There was still no doubt in Anthony's mind that if he took a badger in to Flint, Flint would still fight it — it was all he had been bred and trained to do. However, he was quickly showing everyone that his true nature was calm and peaceful.

'Some people say that dogs like Flint should never be re-homed,' said Anthony. 'That there's too much violence in their past and in their breeding for them ever to be safe pets, and because of their size they have the ability to do real damage. But I, and the staff at the centre, know that this isn't the case — and that despite the myths, studies have shown that dogs bred specifically for fighting are no more aggressive towards people than other dogs. I could see that Flint had a lovely temperament, and that like any dog, as long as he was sensibly re-homed with the right people, he would make a brilliant family pet.'

While Flint was slowly recovering, Anthony was trying to find the culprits who'd almost killed him in such an appalling way. Yet, despite a newspaper and media appeal for information, he heard nothing. The 'dog men' had closed ranks, and there were no leads.

'Whenever I went to see Flint I had two thoughts. One was that I wanted him to spend the rest of his life sitting comfortably on someone's couch. The other was that the culprits behind this cruelty should one day hear the clang of a prison-cell door slamming behind them.'

Anthony's thoughts were echoed by the team that helped bring Flint back to health and happiness but, sadly, there was no justice to be had, and the perpetrators have never been traced.

However, Anthony's first wish for Flint did come true,

and a wonderful happy-ever-after was in store for him. If he'd had a lucky break when Anthony rescued him, he had another one when Mike Garnett and his sixteen-year-old son, Toby, walked into the RSPCA Wirral & Chester Branch Animal Centre, looking for a pet dog.

Mike and his wife, Louise, had always enjoyed walking, and Mike frequently walked with a friend who owned dogs. It made the couple think that it would be nice to have a little dog of their own, and Toby was really keen. He'd been asking for a dog ever since they'd lost their cat six months earlier, and the house felt empty without a pet.

Mike and Toby had agreed they wanted a rescue dog, and when they saw a small terrier on the RSPCA website they went to the Wirral & Chester Branch Animal Centre to talk about him. Mike explained that they were looking for a dog for the whole family, including Louise and their eighteen-year-old daughter, Beth, as they would all be involved in looking after him.

Two of the centre staff, Michelle and Mandy, told them they had the perfect dog, although they warned Mike that he was a bit bigger than the terrier they had in mind. When asked if they'd like to have a look at him, they expected to be taken to the kennels, but instead the staff just stepped aside and there, behind them, was a huge dog, Flint, watching them with sad eyes.

'As we looked back he lowered his head, as if to say, "Why would anyone want me?" He had a broken tail – this was before the second operation on it – his face was raw, and he still had wounds all over him, but there was something in his eyes that was irresistible,' remembers Mike.

It's easy to see why the staff felt that Mike and Toby were a good fit for Flint: Mike is six foot five inches tall and Toby is even taller, at six foot eight. Daughter Beth is also over six feet. Mike couldn't help but think that fate had played a hand when they walked in, because the staff could see that they and Flint were really suited to each other.

Just a few moments spent getting to know the gentle giant convinced Mike and Toby that Flint was the dog for them.

'They told us he'd been used as a badger-baiter, but I had no idea what that meant,' Mike recalls. 'When it was explained, my first reaction was to be angry that anyone could do that to him. And I did wonder what sort of pet he would make. But the staff were able to show us how placid he was, how he spent all day on his bed in reception, never getting agitated, taking everything in his stride.'

As is suggested in RSPCA adoption guidelines, Mike went to the centre to spend time with Flint. Louise and Toby were also regular visitors. They accepted that it was very important to give that much time to Flint. The RSPCA's thinking is that if you can't manage to visit the dog you hope to own, how will you care for him every single day when you have him at home?

Before Flint went home, the RSPCA re-homers carefully observed his behaviour when he encountered new people and situations, and other animals, to get to know him as an individual. This was particularly important given his past. It would help to make sure his new home was the right one, and give Mike and the family as much information as possible about his behaviour in the centre.

The family went into adopting Flint with their eyes open, knowing he would change their lives. Beth was the only family member who was slightly unsure about the new arrival, wary of him because of his size. However, that quickly changed as she got to know him. It took only a few days for her to become as big a fan of Flint as the rest of the Garnett family were.

'These days, the minute she walks into the house, she kicks her shoes off, drops her bag, and gets down on the floor with Flint,' says Mike. 'His eyes light up when she comes into the room.'

For the first couple of months, the Garnetts were advised by the RSPCA to keep Flint on a lead while out walking, until he had learnt a reliable recall and would come back to them. The first time he was let off, free to go anywhere he pleased, he was so happy he ran round and round in circles, then tore off up the beach, leaving Mike with no more than a prayer: 'Please, please come back . . .'

'He's an impressive runner, and as I saw him disappearing up the beach, I worried he would keep going. But he turned and came back to me, pleased with himself, and we were both deliriously happy,' says Mike.

In fact, for the first six months after they took Flint home, the Garnetts, who live on the Wirral, only let Flint run off the lead when he was on the beach, where there were no trees or bushes. In parks or fields they kept him on the lead because they were worried he would still chase squirrels or other furry animals — the thing he'd been trained to do for years. Even now, if he sees a cat or a squirrel, he will look up at his owner, seeking confirmation about what to do. It shows how far he's come, though, as it only takes a simple 'no' to quell his instincts.

'Besides, now we've got his weight up, he's too big in the backside to catch anything. He's certainly not as agile as he was . . .' chuckles Mike.

From the moment they adopted Flint, rescuing him from a wretched existence, he has shown himself to be such a quiet, easy-going family pet that it's often hard to believe such cruelty dominated his early years. His torn ear, his lack of teeth, his damaged jaw, the half of his nose that is missing, and the hundreds of tiny scars that can be seen where his dark brown fur has grown back white, are clues to what life was once like for him but, for the most part, his personality seems to have been unaffected by his harsh upbringing.

On his flank, barely discernible now that fur once again covers it, is a half-moon-shaped scar, probably caused when he was hit with a spade or stick to keep him fired up and fighting, or to make sure he didn't escape. Above one of his eyes is another pronounced scar and, yet again, he was lucky that it wasn't half an inch lower, or he would have lost the eye.

Although he now fits in to family life so well, when Flint first moved in to the Garnett family home, there were considerable signs of anxiety – a legacy from his background. He hated being left alone, and so the family hated to leave him, but after slowly and carefully getting him used to being on his own for increasing increments of time, Mike and Louise can now go out for three to four hours and leave him unsupervised in the house, safe in the knowledge that he's happy. There are willing babysitters if they need to be away for longer, with Louise's father or Mike's mother always happy to lend a hand looking after the gentle giant.

Other challenges from the early days include the first time they took him away on holiday, when he seemed nervous, agitated. It was only when he realized the family were staying with him, not leaving him somewhere new and unknown, that he relaxed. They reasoned that he must have been used to being driven to different places to fight, and he was worried that was happening again. The theory was born out when, on one occasion, they took him to Wales, where he had come from. He seemed to sense where he was, and whenever they stopped the car to let him out he was terrified. He calmed down after being petted and reassured by his new, loving family.

He also suffered from vivid nightmares, when he would shake uncontrollably, baring his teeth, his eyes rolling and his legs moving rapidly, as though he were trying to get away from something. A gentle shake and a stroke usually dispelled the unhappy memories, and as time went on, the nightmares diminished and now happen only very occasionally. As the past recedes, the hope is he now has so many good memories to dream about that they have taken over from the bad ones.

Flint certainly has never appeared to take his good luck with his new life for granted, though. Each time he gets back home from a walk, he'll wait by the front doorstep and won't go into the house until invited. Then, with his stumpy tail wagging madly, he'll get straight into his dog bed, or head to the kitchen in the hope of a treat. It brings a lump to the family's throats that this wonderful dog is so touchingly appreciative of his new, happy home.

All the family's lives have been changed by Flint's arrival, but they're in unanimous agreement that the change is for the better. In much the same way that Flint has made so many mental shifts to settle into his new life, so too has the family made physical adjustments to accommodate its newest member. In the beginning, Flint would scratch the carpet whenever he was left alone, so they simply took it up and put down laminate flooring while they helped him overcome his issues.

He's not allowed on the sofa in the living room, but there's an extension at the back of the house, which used to be a playroom when the children were small, and so that's where Flint sleeps. Mike put patio doors in so that he could look outside, as he did in his RSPCA kennel. Then they realized that it was a good room for everyone to enjoy, so they put a sofa and a television in there, and Flint is now allowed to hop up on the couch with Mike when he's watching football.

'It's been a big life change for us, tending to his needs, taking him out three times a day. But we've gained as much as he has. We've met so many people, made new friends and acquaintances through him. Other people talk of not being able to do things because of the dog, but he's fitted in perfectly. I take him to West Kirby beach and, after running up and down it, he's happy to sit by the fire in one of the cafés or wine bars, and he loves other people making a fuss of him.'

He's still slightly nervous of men they meet when they are out. He prefers women on the whole, although he happily accepts men if they have a dog with them. A solitary stranger, or a group of men, also seems to unnerve him and he'll stick very close to Mike. Perhaps because the women at the RSPCA animal centre made such a fuss of him when he was so poorly, he associates kindness with females. And he's clearly known a lot of unkindness from men in the past.

In his new life, Flint enjoys meeting other dogs and never retaliates when he meets an aggressive one. Some owners of small dogs will pick their pets up as he approaches, clearly disconcerted by his size, but when they hear and see that he is gentle they tentatively put their own dogs down and apologize for their initial concern, as Flint gently sniffs around them.

For the first twelve months after being re-homed, Flint couldn't have barked even if he'd wanted to. He didn't make a sound. His throat had been so badly injured in that final fight that he was unable to bark, and it's possible that his voicebox may even have been deliberately damaged by his previous owners to stop him barking while fighting, which would draw attention to the illegal activity. These days, he's able to utter a low, guttural howl, which he does in the morning when he hears the family are awake upstairs.

'He's telling us that he's awake, too. He was toilet trained when we got him, but once had an accident in the night and messed in the house. When I came downstairs, he was cowering in the corner of the kitchen — he was clearly expecting to be beaten. He'd even tried to make sure that he'd made his mess on the kitchen paper we put on the floor near his bowls. It broke my heart to think that he was frightened. I said to him, "Don't worry, mate. What have you been through in the past?" I gave him a big fuss to show him he was still loved.'

He reminds the Garnetts that he likes his breakfast at 7.30 a.m., and food is very important to him because he was half-starved when he was rescued. He dances excitedly when his meals are being prepared. However, his love of food means the family has to keep an eye on him when they go out, because he'll eat anything he comes across, though even this can be endearing. Most of his missing teeth are from one side of his mouth, which means he slobbers and drools whenever he's eating or drinking.

'When he shakes his head his tongue comes flying out, and it's so long it hits him on the back of his head. He doesn't realize what's happened, and he looks round, puzzled to see what hit him, which is really funny to see,' says Mike with a smile.

It's easy to see why Flint makes an impression wherever he goes, and not just because of his size. He's good at remembering people, making friends and building relationships. When the Garnetts take Flint back to the veterinary practice where Holly, who first treated him, is based there's a cacophony of greetings. All the staff queue up to say 'Hello, Flint' and give their old friend a fuss.

His relationship with each of the Garnetts is equally strong and unique, and he gives them all every bit as much as they give him. Louise naturally walks more slowly than her long-legged husband, for instance, and so whenever she and Flint go out together, Flint acknowledges the difference in pace and stays at her side, happy to be protective of her.

'When Michelle at the RSPCA said she had the perfect dog for us, she couldn't have got it more right,' confirms Mike happily, but behind the smiles there's also some quiet sadness. The Garnetts know that, because of his size and his injuries, Flint may not live a long life and may only have been gifted to them for a short time, so they do their best to make the most of every day with him. All they want is for him to enjoy the rest of his life in comfort and without any worries. It's something he deserves after all he's been through.

Six weeks after Flint moved into the family home, the Garnetts experienced a brutal reminder of Flint's previous history. As Toby was taking him out for a walk across some neighbouring fields, two men drove past in a van. The vehicle braked suddenly before reversing back up the street. The men jumped out and rapidly crossed the field to confront Toby and Flint.

'Your dog's worth a lot of money, you want to watch yourself,' they said menacingly, before grabbing Flint, as though to take him away. Luckily, the combination of Toby's size and the timely arrival of a group of his friends meant the boys were able to chase the men off.

In any case, the men seemed to lose interest in Flint once they saw he'd been castrated and had lost so many teeth, including his front ones.

'What the hell have you done? He's no good to anyone. You've ruined him,' they scoffed.

Having spotted Flint across the field, they clearly thought he'd be a good fighting dog — big and strong, they knew he could be trained to fight. It's not uncommon for approaches to be made to people who have adopted big dogs like Flint from the RSPCA.

As soon as he heard Toby's account of the encounter, Mike rang Anthony, who was fairly sure he knew who the two men were. Since Flint's rescue, he'd managed successfully to bring about the prosecution of four men from his local area for badger-baiting crimes, and he suspected that these two men were part of that gang. He told Mike and his family that if they were ever approached again, the very first thing they should say is that Flint has been castrated. The gangs who use these dogs to fight want them intact, believing that it makes them fight harder, and also because they can use them for breeding.

Anthony believes that sadly the 'sport' of badger-baiting is not in decline; on the contrary, the perpetrators are becoming increasingly brazen. He estimates that there are thousands of 'dog men' in England and Wales, making his job of keeping dogs safe from harm that much more difficult. He points to Flint's story as a good case in point. Flint's abusers were on a playing field next to a school, with houses near by. They used to operate out in the countryside, covertly, in secluded places, but now they're training their dogs in plain sight, in local parks.

'That's why,' he says, 'it's important that we catch them, and that the courts take the crime seriously and ensure they're sent to prison.' It's a subject close to his heart.

'There are hunting forums on the internet where these lads compare the specifics of dogs, such as their bloodline, hardness and what quarry they're suitable for. They deliberately keep them short of food – just enough to give them optimum speed and stamina but not enough to diminish their strength.

'Occasionally they turn the dogs on farm livestock. They don't do it for food to eat, or to control problem species. They do it for their own twisted gratification, taking videos of it for bragging rights. It's one of the most frustrating forms of cruelty I deal with, because it's institutionalized. We see lads as young as fourteen or fifteen, bred into it by their fathers. It's almost always lads and men, although there is, very occasionally, a female involved.

'The injuries these dogs suffer are horrendous. They won't take the dogs to a vet, because any honourable, self-respecting vet would treat them but then inform the RSPCA or the police. So they treat the dogs' wounds themselves: there's often one man who specializes in patching up dogs. I've seen dogs who had wounds stapled together with ordinary staples, or stitched with fishing line. They buy dodgy antibiotics on the internet. Unfortunately, there are also one or two dodgy vets who will treat badger dogs and ask no questions. They should be ashamed of themselves. Although giving the dogs treatment is a good thing, by turning a blind eye they're letting the dogs walk back into more cruelty, and they're doing nothing to help stamp it out.'

Catching the 'dog men' is difficult, as the community they operate in closes ranks around them and protects them. It means that appeals for information often result in nothing – no one dares to come forward. So when Anthony is able to assist in getting arrests and convictions, he's thrilled.

The four men the RSPCA managed to get into court on badger-baiting offences had six injured dogs in the back of their van when they were apprehended, some of the animals seriously hurt. The men claimed they'd been hunting rabbits and that the dogs had attacked a fox accidentally, and that was the cause of their horrible injuries. However, on one of their phones, Anthony and his team found sickening video footage of a badger and a fox being attacked – really shocking images accompanied by the sound of the men laughing in the background.

'It's enough to make you despair of humanity. These men

are the lowest of the low, and I'm very happy to see them go to prison, even if the sentences aren't long enough for the suffering they've caused to wildlife and to the dogs they profess to care about.'

In this particular case, one of the men got twenty-two weeks in jail, one received a sentence of sixteen weeks, and the other two, twelve weeks. When a prosecution is successful, for a while at least, dogs like Flint are a little bit safer.

Anthony cares deeply about all the dogs he rescues – each and every one gets under his skin – but he admits there is something very special about Flint. The bond established in a field in Wales, when the dog was at his lowest ebb, has never been broken. Even from a distance Flint still recognizes the man who saved him, and takes off at great speed to be reunited with him. His stump of a tail wags as fast as it can, and he presses his considerable weight against Anthony's legs.

'He's a very special dog,' says Anthony with a smile. 'And he's got a special place in my heart.'

TIPS ON HOW TO CARE FOR YOUR DOG

Choosing the right breed

DOGS VARY in size and shape more than any other pet animal, even within breeds — there are more than 340 breeds worldwide, and nearly 220 recognized in the UK — so this is an important consideration when choosing a dog. Some types of dog can grow into adults weighing as much as 70kg. However, whatever their size, shape or breed, all dogs need space to exercise, play and rest undisturbed.

While some people may have a breed, size or sex of dog that they prefer, it's important to remember that every dog is unique and has their own personality. How a dog or puppy behaves and fits into a family will depend on how they are treated and trained, as well as on their character and temperament. It's a mix of nurture and nature.

It's therefore really important not to generalize that all dogs of a breed have the same characteristics. A dog's personality and behaviour is known to be affected by their breed, but these natural tendencies can be substantially altered by the way in which the dog is reared. The range of environmental experiences and human interactions to which a dog is exposed is extremely important in shaping a dog's behaviour. A lack of, or inappropriate, experiences during development can have a detrimental effect on adult behaviour.

▶

If you're considering adding a dog to your family, it's always worth considering re-homing one of the many dogs in rescue centres looking for their forever home. There are dogs of all shapes, sizes and personalities looking for homes. Qualified staff will help you to choose the right dog for your circumstances. If you're thinking about buying a puppy privately, always use the puppy contract — a free document that helps ensure that you are buying a content, healthy puppy who has been bred and reared with the best chance of living a long, happy life, and being a well-adjusted adult. The contract is free to download from www.puppycontract.org.uk.

CHAPTER 5

Ted

As RSPCA Inspector Jo Daniel says, more than 90 per cent of her work as an inspector is about helping and advising animal owners. It's not about taking animals away from them. Usually, owners who care about their pets will act on advice, get the correct veterinary help, make sure they serve up the right amount of suitable food and, in the case of dogs especially, get them outside for exercise and toileting. Ignorance is the biggest problem the RSPCA deals with, not wilful cruelty. However, sometimes there comes a point when action has to be taken. In the case of Ted, and the other pets in his home, it wasn't the physical state of the animals that worried Jo as much as the squalid conditions in which they were living.

The tiny bedsit where Ted was living looked as if it had been ransacked. Piles of clothes, discarded packaging, food waste, overturned furniture, soiled bedding and animal faeces were strewn across the floor. Living in the mess were two dogs, two cats and two caged birds, as well as their owner, a young man who was out at work for long hours every day, leaving the animals alone in the squalor.

Jo knew the address well – she'd been there several times before. In fact, for twelve months she'd been working with the owner to improve conditions but over the course of the year, instead of getting better, the state of the flat had gone downhill, and Jo had become more and more concerned about the animals' welfare.

The man misguidedly believed he was helping the poor creatures he took in. Ironically, he was operating his own chaotic animal 'rescue' project, but from the most impractical premises, and in the time Jo had been monitoring the flat, there had been a transient population of different animals, some of them brought in from abroad. The man was trying to get them fostered and re-homed, and genuinely thought it was his mission to save them. He wasn't intentionally ill-treating or deliberately neglecting the animals, but he didn't have space for them in a one-room flat with only a small kitchenette and bathroom. His job required him to be elsewhere a lot of the time, so he had no time to exercise the dogs, and obviously wasn't coping with looking after them all, or even able to keep his own living space in a habitable condition.

Since Jo's first visit, the number of animals had declined from four dogs, five cats and four caged birds, but nevertheless the state of the flat had deteriorated appallingly, and it was clear from the faeces littering the floor that the dogs weren't getting outside at all. After two warning notices from Jo made no difference and conditions worsened further, the RSPCA inspector felt she had no option but to remove all the animals.

As sometimes happens, the young man refused to sign the animals over to the RSPCA, and in the distraught confrontation that followed, Jo had to call out the police to help her remove them, due to the serious animal welfare concerns. She was particularly worried about the two dogs: Ted, a very boisterous, wild young male, and an older, inquisitive and friendly bitch called Amber. They were both springer spaniels, often lively and energetic dogs needing large amounts of exercise, which they simply weren't getting. Cooped up in the tiny flat, they must have been intensely bored, miserable and understimulated, with no means of indulging their natural enthusiasm for life.

Their excess energy was apparent as Jo led them out of the flat, bouncing on the end of their leads, to her waiting van. They both had minor skin problems, had suffered a small amount of fur loss from spending too long in an enclosed space, and were a little bit underweight, but otherwise were in good health. They were by no means one of the worst cases that Jo has faced in her twenty-two years as an inspector, but she had no doubt that they were in distress and suffering in that flat. Whether the owner liked it or not, she'd had to make a decision that focused on their, and the other animals', well-being and needs being met.

When the animals arrived at the RSPCA West Hatch Animal Centre near Taunton in Somerset, they were each checked over by a vet. It was then that Jo and the staff at the centre discovered that Ted had found at least one way to use his time in the restricted space of the bedsit: Amber was pregnant, and it seemed more than likely that he was the father.

Sue Dicks, the supervisor at the West Hatch centre, has worked there for twenty years, and has seen countless dogs, cats, birds, rabbits and more exotic pets re-homed, going on to lead happy lives with owners who understand their needs. It's a fulfilling job, and Sue loves it, though during that time, she's also found another role for herself.

More than ten years ago she came across a particularly bright, energetic, intelligent spaniel that had been brought in, and it seemed to her that he would make a great working dog. She tentatively contacted her local police force to see what their requirements were for training dogs to work in the police dog unit, and that call was the start of a long and very fruitful relationship. Since then, Sue has passed fifteen dogs on to the police for training, and nothing pleases her more than seeing an animal that has come into the centre as a result of neglect or cruelty moving on to a busy, fulfilled working life with a police handler who gives them all the stimulation and affection they need.

For the past ten years she has worked closely with PC Lee Webb, who runs the training of dogs for the combined forces of Avon and Somerset Police, Wiltshire Police and Gloucestershire Police, and he has had a lot of input into how she screens potential police dogs.

The first thing Sue does when she meets any young, active dog is to play around with them in the centre's compound, to see initially if they have a good all-round personality, and are friendly and confident, not needy or withdrawn. She'll throw a ball, and some dogs are simply not interested in fetching it for her. There will be others, however, who are focused and enthusiastic, despite everything they've been through. For these dogs, she'll start to throw the ball into difficult areas, such as thickets of vegetation, and will then progress to hiding the ball up a tree to see if they'll stand beneath the tree, alerting her to where the ball is. If all continues to go well, and the dog seems keen and happy, she'll start hiding the ball in the centre's workshop, or the garage, and eventually in her own car, increasing the challenge each time.

If a dog is still keen on finding the hidden ball, Sue puts in a call to Lee, alerting him to a dog he might be interested in having a look at. Then it's Lee's turn to put the dog through some basic paces, playing the same games with the ball that Sue has already been doing, and making his own assessment.

Soon after Ted and Amber arrived at the centre, Sue could see tremendous potential in Ted, a white-and-brown dog, with brown face and ears and a flash of white down his nose, a large brown spot on his back, and a brown-and-white tail. Amber, too, was a very focused, willing, inquisitive dog, but at an estimated four or five years old, she was too old for training, and she was also carrying her puppies. So Sue concentrated on Ted, who the vet thought was about a year old, and Lee went down to meet him at the smallholding where Sue lives.

They took him out for a long walk with Sue's own dog, a Rottweiler by the name of Sobek, and Sue demonstrated how Ted would search for a ball in a haystack, hidden on the back of a lorry, and in the chassis of a tractor. Lee could see that as well as being keen to find the ball, Ted also got on well with other dogs — not just Sobek but the ones at the centre — and was also good with people.

He agreed with Sue that Ted initially looked like a suitable dog to train, cautiously adding that this inquisitiveness was just the first requirement, and that for Ted to join the ranks of the 1,800 police dogs in the UK, he would need to go through a rigorous six-week training programme. As for a handler, Lee knew just the right police officer to take on Ted.

PC Sam Dutton, of Wiltshire Police, had been with the dog unit for just over a year, working with Chico, a German shepherd, as her 'general purpose' dog, who can be used for crowd control, searching people, tracking people and finding items such as mobile phones that criminals discard when being chased but which still carry their scent. After twelve months on the team, dog handlers are given the option to apply for another, specialist sniffer dog, trained either to detect explosives or drugs, firearms and cash. Sam had put in her application to work with another dog, and Lee was sure she would be a good match for Ted.

Just before her first meeting with Ted, Lee sprang the news on Sam that, for the first time ever, a camera crew had been given access to the training that she and Ted were about to receive, all the way through the six-week course. Sam was grateful for the heads-up.

'It'll be fine, we know you've got a sense of humour,' Lee reassured her.

She was happy to agree to being filmed, though, because she wanted to spread the word about how great rescued dogs can be.

Sam joined the police in 2004, having worked for them as a civilian for four years previously. She always wanted to join the dog unit, because she grew up with and loved dogs, but before she was transferred to the unit she worked as a community beat manager in the domestic abuse unit, and spent time on major investigations teams. There's a long wait to work with dogs, as it's such a popular division, and Sam was thrilled when she was finally accepted for the unit. It's a demanding job, as she's responsible for her dogs all the time, even when she's off duty. She needs to be willing and able to care for them around the clock.

Her first encounter with Ted went better than she expected,

Above: Timmy, out on a walk with housemates Lucky and Max.

Below: Timmy enjoying the great outdoors.

Left: Clover and Tanya having a cuddle.

Above: Lurcher Lily, pretty in pink.

Below: Lily with her owners Hazel and John Catt, and Maureen.

Top: Flint goes for a paddle.

Above: Smiles all round — Mike and Louise Garnett, with Flint.

Left: Flint with Anthony: 'He's got a special place in my heart.'

Above: The irrepressible Ted retrieves a tennis ball.

Right: PC Sam Dutton and her sniffer dog Ted take a well-deserved break.

Bottom: Handsome, intelligent, loving and gentle Eddie.

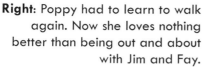

Above: Reo — 'It was a no-brainer for us,' says Martin Corrin.

Below: The Corrins with Reo and Anthony. Re-homing staff had feared that Reo would struggle to find a forever home.

Above left: Molly, the little white terrier, wraps up after a warm bath.

Above right: Molly with Amanda Hull: 'She's my little ray of sunshine.'

Below: Molly is full of beans and loves being outside.

Above left: Buddy and his best friend Max. They are devoted to each other.

Above right: Buddy and Max take a road trip: 'He's our lovely boy,' says Wendy Ehlen.

Below: Anthony and Lauren Harrison, with Ruby: 'I just wanted to give her a good life, to make up for what had happened to her.'

and he took to her straight away. She didn't know his history, except that he'd been rescued by the RSPCA and his previous owner was being prosecuted (and was subsequently banned from keeping animals for ten years). Despite Sam's initial worries that smaller dogs might be more independent, less willing to work closely with people, and that she would have to try harder to establish a bond with her new dog, the minute the two met and Ted bounded up to her, it was clear to everyone that this wasn't the case and they were going to get on and become a team – just as long as Ted managed to get through the rigorous training course.

The next hurdle was introducing Ted to Sam's other dogs, first and foremost Chico, who was three-and-a-half years old at the time, and not a very sociable animal. Sam and her partner, Matt, who is a police community support officer, have three other dogs: Quinn, an elderly lurcher who was thirteen at the time he first met Ted; Isla, a six-year-old sprocker (springer-cocker spaniel cross); and Koda, a young springer the same age as Ted.

Sam was worried that Chico wouldn't take to his new companion. Her other three dogs are pets who live in the house, but the two police dogs were to be kennelled next to one another outside in the garden, in adjacent, super, two-storey kennels. Sam initially wondered whether they would have to be separated, but after a few meetings supervised by Sam and Lee, Chico accepted his new, enthusiastic young colleague. It was difficult for anyone to resist outgoing and friendly Super Ted.

A hangover from Ted's past makes him very protective about his food, and when Sam goes to the outbuilding where she stores the dog food, he follows her and refuses to allow any of the other dogs to get near. Sam feeds them all separately, so it's not a problem that Ted has a need to supervise his feeding time, and she feels lucky that this seems to be the only behavioural legacy of his miserable past. It could, she recognizes, be so much worse.

'He's very confident, loves to be around people, takes new environments in his stride, and he doesn't seem to have any hang-ups. He's full of himself.'

At first Ted was a bit too full of himself with Sam's other dogs and those he met on walks, because, she thinks, he'd never had the chance to play before he was rescued. He could be a little too boisterous and needed to be 'told off' once or twice by other dogs. He soon learned that not all dogs are as young, friendly and up for play as he is.

When Sam first met Ted, there were still one or two areas on his body where his fur hadn't grown back fully, and where he'd clearly been licking. Now, to minimize any irritation to his sensitive skin, he's fed an allergen-free diet, Sam washes him with a medicated shampoo, is careful to make sure he has the right hypoallergenic bedding, and she washes it with a dermatologically tested soap powder for sensitive skin.

Most police dogs go to work wearing harnesses that tell members of the public they are working police dogs, but Sam soon discovered that Ted's harness made his sensitive skin inflamed and sore. Instead, he now works wearing a collar, which doesn't irritate his skin, with the word 'police' on it.

Having settled in at home with Sam's other dogs, it was time for Ted to start training in earnest. Because police dogs have to work in environments they've never encountered before, surrounded by unfamiliar objects, the first task, even before he could be given a place on the course, was to put Ted in a strange room to see how quickly he acclimatized.

Initially he was disturbed by an office chair on wheels, which he'd clearly never come across before, but after exploring it thoroughly and identifying it as an inanimate object, he moved on to investigating the boxes, furniture and work surfaces. Police sniffer dogs are actively encouraged to leap up everywhere and sniff about in cupboards, in contrast to pet dogs living with a family, who are often told to keep off the furniture and kitchen work surfaces. Ted quickly showed he could retrieve his favourite tennis ball when it was in a sink or enclosed in a box, and Lee was enthusiastic about the way he used his nose in the search, not just his eyes.

After a successful observation, Lee was happy to tell Sam that she and her new canine companion had places on the sniffer-dog training course. As they waited to start, Sam concentrated on building the natural bond between her and Ted: she groomed him, played with him, took him on long walks, and simply spent time with him. There was a lot riding on how they worked as a team. If Ted failed the course, he'd be re-homed outside the police, and Sam would lose the little fella who'd already become one of her best friends. The thought of him failing was very worrying, but at this stage there was a long way to go and, despite her innate optimism, Sam was taking it one day at a time. She'd fallen in love with Ted from day one, but had to keep telling herself to be prepared to let him go if it didn't work out in training.

Dogs' noses contain two million more scent receptors than ours. Since human beings have tapped into this resource, the canine nose has proved indispensable in many fields, including search and rescue, sometimes in extreme and dangerous conditions. Dogs can also use their sense of smell to warn of imminent problems in people with diabetes, and can detect some kinds of cancer from urine samples. The fight against crime is just one important way in which dogs, with their amazing noses, have proved invaluable.

At the beginning of his training, Ted was introduced to the

scent of three different illegal drugs: amphetamines, cocaine and ecstasy, which were initially presented to him along with his favourite tennis ball, which he'd been successfully sniffing out wherever it was hidden. The ball was later removed, and Ted showed that he could still find the drugs. He'd come to recognize that he wasn't just seeking his ball, but the drugs too. Then, the ball and its smell could be removed and he was still willing and able to seek the scent of the drugs.

As part of the course, Lee showed Sam how to use clicker training, a very effective way of telling dogs, with a click, when they have achieved the right result. It's a good technique to use for pet dogs, too, but especially useful with highly specialized work, and not a method Sam had ever used before.

The next phase of training involved finding each of the three drugs individually, and at first Ted struggled with the amphetamines, although he easily found the other two. A little bit more input from Sam and Lee was necessary, giving extra training on this elusive scent, until he began to recognize it every time and was up to scratch.

Ted showed how good a sniffer dog he was becoming by successfully finding drugs hidden in a builder's skip full of rubbish, although he was temporarily diverted by an old sandwich someone had thrown away. This was in the early days of training, however, and now he completely ignores food when he's working. Despite his continued fixation with food at mealtimes, he's been trained to focus only on the smells he's searching for when he's in work mode.

The next phase of his training saw Ted finding drugs where they were present only in very small amounts. With this mastered, he moved on to an even trickier part of the job: finding firearms, or parts of firearms. Drugs give off more scent than metal firearms, but dogs can detect tiny amounts of gunpowder residue left on guns, and Lee made sure that Ted was successfully trained on guns that had been fired just once, so they had only a minute smell trace.

When it came to testing his new skills, Ted was up against two experienced sniffer dogs, who were going through their routine in-service appraisals. Sam was bursting with pride when her little waggy-tailed mate, the rescue dog who'd had such a difficult start, outperformed one of the older dogs, finding different firearm parts in a first-aid box, under a fridge, hanging on a coat peg, and hidden in another box. He even excelled at the most difficult test of all: finding drugs stashed inside a vacuum cleaner, among the dust and all the many other distracting smells. Lee was very impressed – this was a really difficult task and one of the other, more experienced dogs failed it.

At every stage, Ted was expected to find his target objects in unfamiliar locations. So far, so good.

From time to time, Lee takes his trainee sniffer-dog handlers to West Hatch Animal Centre to use their premises for searches. Sam and Ted's visit coincided with the re-homing of some of the seven puppies that Ted's former flatmate Amber had given birth to. Ted, who is almost certainly their father, was able to meet them, and he licked them tenderly, as if he realized his connection to them.

Everything was going very well with Ted's training, and Sam was looking forward to, in her words, 'getting on with the job of catching criminals'. However, just around the corner was a major setback, one that nearly ended Ted's embryonic career as a sniffer dog, and which could have put him back in the animal centre looking for a new home.

Ted's irrepressible exuberance and love of his work meant

that everywhere he went, his tail would be wagging at a rate of knots, bashing against any hard surface it came into contact with. After searching enthusiastically through vehicles, rooms and undergrowth, day after day, the tip of Ted's tail soon started to split and bleed. After every search, the walls of the premises would be splattered with his blood. Sam cleaned the wound, treated it with antibiotic cream and applied a bandage, but the next time Ted went to work and his tail began to thrash again at speed, it took only a few seconds for the dressing to be discarded. A plastic sheath for his tail also came off too easily, and it was clear the injury was causing him pain, which in turn was diminishing his amazing focus on the job. Ted's future career was in jeopardy, and Sam was devastated.

Eager for the RSPCA to once again come to the rescue of super-spaniel Ted, she took him back to the RSPCA centre at West Hatch, to see if a vet would agree to operate and remove the injured part of Ted's tail.

'I literally begged them to help us. I knew that without the op, Teddy's career was over before it even began and he'd be in a lot of pain,' she recalls. 'I was desperate for them to see that it was a medical necessity. The RSPCA agreed, and were willing to pay for the operation.'

Reducing the length of a dog's tail is illegal unless it's done for medical reasons or the dog is used in law enforcement, and it's not an operation a vet will undertake without good reason. When vet Amy Colling saw Ted she, too, was happy for the tip of his tail to be amputated. Sam was utterly delighted to hear that Amy agreed that Ted had a chronic, non-healing wound, and needed a few inches removed from his tail. Although it's a last-resort operation, it can be necessary to stop pain and further damage.

Amy and Sam discussed which vertebra in Ted's tail

would mark the point of amputation, and they agreed it would be nice if he could have a small tuft of white hair at the end of his shorter tail. After giving Ted an anaesthetic, Amy applied a tourniquet below the chosen vertebra to reduce blood loss, and then cut through a joint in the vertebra, stitching it up afterwards. The operation involved removing about 40 per cent of his tail, but that still left him, in Amy's words, 'with a good amount of tail to wag'.

Sam was delighted to be reunited with her plucky little mate when he drowsily came round after the operation, greeting him with a warm-hearted, 'Hello, little man. Don't worry, I'll look after you, kid.'

Ted made a rapid recovery from the surgery, but for the first ten days, while he waited for his stitches to be removed, he couldn't go back into his outside kennel at Sam and Matt's home. His operation coincided with Matt recovering from a round of chemotherapy – to combat bladder cancer which, thankfully, has been successfully treated – so Matt and Ted lay on the sofa together, recuperating, while Sam went out to work with Chico.

After being spoilt by the warmth of the house and the comfort of the sofa during his recovery, Sam worried that Ted might be reluctant to return to the more austere conditions of his kennel, and felt sad transferring him back there. She needn't have worried. Again, he demonstrated his ability to take everything in his bouncing stride, and was more than happy to move outside if it meant getting back to going out with Sam every day.

Resuming the training course, Ted continued to do very well, and after six weeks reached the day of his final examination. PC Avery, an independent assessor, watched Sam put him through his paces, finding drugs, firearms and hidden wads of cash in unfamiliar places. Both dog and handler were on trial and Sam was nervous, but confident Ted would pull it off. Lee, who had been with Ted on his journey from the moment Sue rang him to alert him to the existence of another possible sniffer dog, also came along to the assessment for moral support, and as a show of his faith in the duo.

Everything was going very well, with Ted getting through four of his five challenges with only one small hiccup, for which Sam takes the blame. A gun was hidden behind a roller shutter and Ted had been showing Sam he was interested in that part of the room. It wasn't until Sam released the shutter and pulled it up a little way, though, that Ted was able to clearly alert Sam to the gun's presence. It was a lesson for Sam – she should have acted sooner – and when she tells the story of the assessment she insists on exonerating her little mate.

It was then time for the pair to face their final challenge, one that Ted had sailed through many times in training, and one that both Sam and Lee were sure he would pull off without a hitch: searching for drugs in an abandoned car. To their dismay, Ted seemed totally unable to focus, and was completely distracted. It became apparent that a very territorial robin had made his home in the abandoned car, and the bird's aggressive behaviour completely threw Ted off the job in hand. It was hugely disappointing for Sam, as well as for trainer Lee, as they both knew Ted was capable of a far better performance.

Sam was completely taken aback. Ted had never lost concentration in training and they had tested him with livestock around, and even in an area adjacent to a pheasant shoot taking place. Until then, distractions had never fazed Ted. Disappointingly, it meant that he failed to get his sniffer dog licence that particular day, but PC Avery was happy to let them come back the following day for another vehicle search.

Although she was bitterly disappointed that things hadn't gone to plan, Sam felt hugely relieved that they were being given another chance. She knew that Ted was up to the task; that he could do everything required of him without putting a foot wrong. So although the day ended in a huge anti-climax, she was hopeful that Ted could redeem himself. The stakes were high. If things went awry again, she knew that he would be sidelined as a sniffer dog and would be on his way back to the animal centre without her.

The confidence she and Lee placed in Ted was amply rewarded the following day when he confidently found keta-mine, an anaesthetic used illegally as a hallucinogen, under the gearstick in the centre of the car's interior, and, even more impressively, mephedrone, an illegal synthetic psycho-active drug, hidden under the car's bonnet.

'This is a totally different dog from the one I saw yester-day,' PC Avery commented. 'He's got great concentration and he's finding the drugs without his handler having to task him.'

Ted's performance was enough to give him and Sam their coveted sniffer dog licence, and Ted was able to take his place in Sam's van, alongside Chico, to go out working with her every day.

When the TV programmes following Ted's training were broadcast, Sam's 'lovely' friends and family inundated her with cards bearing pictures of robins. Every Christmas card that plopped through the letterbox featured a cheerful, red-breasted bird, none of them looking as if they could morph into an aggressive, territorial creature that could disconcert a brilliant little sniffer dog.

Sam and Ted are now inseparable, and Ted and Chico play together happily when she takes them for walks, which is more than she ever expected.

'I am so lucky. I go to work every day with my best friends, I spend all day with them — and they always agree with me! It's a fantastic job — although at three o'clock in the morning in the middle of a field, up to my knees in mud, when it's chucking it down with rain, I may not feel quite so enthusiastic . . .'

Since he started work, Ted has searched for a gun in a murder inquiry, and searches vehicles for drugs, cash and firearms on a regular basis when traffic police stop a known dealer's car. He has searched cells in both HMP Bristol and HMP Erlestoke for drugs, and has found caches of cannabis, cocaine and crack cocaine, as well as stashes of cash in different premises. He's behaved impeccably, even when the residents at the houses he has been searching have been difficult and aggressive.

He's also worked as an ambassador for the police, going into schools, scout groups and to meet police cadets with Sam when she gives talks about the dangers of illegal drugs and the work of the unit. He also goes into every police station Sam visits, to say hello, while Chico, who doesn't take kindly to strangers, stays in the van.

Back at the dog unit base at Wiltshire Police headquarters, Ted proves that he really deserves the name 'springer', by jumping on to the top of the high mesh fence around the dog runs. At home he can also leap on to the top of a high gate meant to keep the dogs in, but he clearly knows how lucky he is and has never leapt down the other side or gone off without permission: he simply uses his high perches as vantage points to survey the world, as if to keep an eye on everything and ensure all is well.

Every six weeks Ted and all the other sniffer dogs are tested so that high standards are maintained, and once a year they go through a more rigorous assessment with their handlers to renew their licences. Ted has sailed through each and every evaluation. As things stand, he'll probably work until he's about ten years old, providing he doesn't develop any serious health problems. When he retires, he'll move inside to join Sam and Matt's pet dogs. Sam knows it will be an 'interesting' time, retraining a dog who's been encouraged to jump all over a room for most of his life, and who has no boundaries to keep his feet off the furniture. She also knows that Ted will be up to the challenge.

Sue Dicks, who first spotted Ted's potential, couldn't be more pleased that he has found a new and very worthwhile life as a police dog. She is still busy spotting new recruits for Lee, and has had success persuading him that some rescue dogs, who may not look like natural sniffer dogs, are well up to the task. Rescue centres across the country are full of Staffordshire bull terriers and other bull breeds, who sometimes get a bad press when they're used by criminals as guard dogs or attack dogs, or for organized fighting. However, Sue has found that many of them also have good noses, a good temperament and a very focused drive to work, and Lee is happy to assess any dog with those qualities. In fact, he now has several Staffies and Staffie crosses working in the dog unit, or undergoing training.

As for RSPCA Inspector Jo Daniel, she is thrilled by Ted's new and very happy life.

'Neglecting a dog isn't just about not feeding it and caring for it. It's also about not recognizing its potential, and giving it the opportunity to exercise and use its brain. Ted was saved from miserable boredom and now he's adored, cared for and performing a great public service. It makes me feel my job is very worthwhile – and so is the job that Ted is now doing.'

TIPS ON HOW TO CARE FOR YOUR DOG

Dogs and their noses

FOR HUMANS, our primary sense is sight, but for dogs it is smell. The average dog has a sense of smell up to 100,000 times more sensitive than ours, and for specialist sniffer dogs it is much higher. A lot of the information they get about their environment comes from olfactory cues, so they spend a lot of time gathering that information by sniffing — which explains why your dog often has his nose to the ground.

Scent is also an important communication tool for dogs. They use it to find out about their world, for example, which other animals and human beings are in their vicinity, and to find food. They also broadcast who and where they are via scents, and do this by depositing various scent markers (urine, faeces and body odour from scent glands) as they go about their daily business. It's a bit like us leaving a note for someone — we don't have to be there to tell them the information.

A lot of this scent activity goes unnoticed by humans because we don't rely on our sense of smell in the same way. For example, having familiar-smelling bedding and toys in a new environment can help a dog settle in and cope better with their unfamiliar surroundings.

Dogs are active and need regular opportunities to exercise in order to keep them fit and stimulated.

▶

However, exercise is not only important in that it provides physical activity, it also provides opportunities for exploration and interaction with people and other dogs. Giving them the chance to use their sense of smell every day can help them keep mentally engaged. 'Find the treat' is a good game to play — hide lots of treats around the house and garden, and get your dog to sniff them out. They get to use their nose, it keeps them busy, and it gets you moving, too.

CHAPTER 6

Eddie

For the sake of £38, Eddie, a handsome, intelligent, loving and gentle dog, was condemned to months of horrific suffering. It was the worst case of a dog with a crippling skin condition that RSPCA Inspector Nick Wheelhouse had ever seen, and the indelible image of Eddie's damaged skin is a memory that will stay with him for ever. Raw, open wounds covered his body, lumps of fur and tissue were hanging off, his eyes and ears were badly infected, and each and every movement he made caused him acute misery.

When Eddie arrived at vet Sonya Miller-Smith's practice,

she shared Nick's anguish at the horrific sight. Was Eddie too far gone to be helped? Was it ethically right to put a dog who was in so much pain through treatment? Would it be kinder simply to ease him tenderly into oblivion, finally freeing him from the agonizing pain that had dominated his last few months – a pain that could have stopped him from sleeping, left him terrified at the idea of being touched on his inflamed, cracked and bleeding body, so covered with suppurating wounds that no part of him was clear? These were the questions that raced through Sonya's mind.

It was impossible to tell whether Eddie was old or young, or even what breed he was. It was clear, however, that demodectic mites had caused an inflammatory reaction that had made the skin itchy and raw-looking. The heartbreak for Sonya and her staff was that this common skin condition could have been successfully treated with an £8 medication and the £30 cost of a visit to the vet, if only Eddie's owner had taken him for treatment when the pup first showed signs of itchiness. Yet he had been left, for months, and the mites had taken control and consumed the skin and tissue all over his body.

It defied belief that anyone could have watched his shocking state deteriorate and not sought treatment for him. Even if Eddie's owner didn't have the money to cover the vet bill, free and discounted treatment is available from the PDSA (the People's Dispensary for Sick Animals) for eligible people and, as Sonya says, no vet should turn away an animal in dire need of treatment and an owner who desperately wants help for their pet.

Nick first heard about the dog – who was named Eddie by Sonya and her staff – when a member of the public phoned him early one January to report a stray with a really bad skin condition. The man claimed he'd found the dog on

Christmas Eve, when he'd been walking his own dog, and that the stray had followed him home. Very concerned about what he'd heard, Nick went directly to the address, where he saw Eddie for the first time, and was shocked to his core. Skin conditions are common in dogs, and often owners simply need advice on how to treat them, but this was such an extreme case. Nick had never encountered an infection so severe.

The man and his partner claimed to have been looking after the dog since they found him, about ten days previously. The man explained that he'd rung the local dog wardens, but they wouldn't come out to help him. So when the pet shops reopened after Christmas, he'd bought an off-the-shelf treatment to stop dog itching, and had been rubbing talcum powder into the dog's open wounds. Nick flinched as he heard this 'remedy' described: it was clear even to someone with no veterinary qualifications that talcum powder would have made the pain and suffering worse, and done absolutely nothing to ease the underlying problem.

Just getting out of the flat was a terrible ordeal for Eddie. Nick coaxed him outside gently, but it was clear that every step was excruciatingly painful, as his damaged skin cracked open with every move. The poor animal didn't make a sound, not a whimper nor a moan. He seemed, to Nick, completely defeated; a dog so downtrodden that he really just didn't want to go on.

As the front door closed behind the pair, the heavens opened and rain came down in torrents. Little Eddie didn't flinch, although the raindrops must have stung as they struck his open wounds.

'It was as if nothing worse or more painful could happen to him. He'd gone beyond the limits of endurance,' said Nick.

Getting Eddie into the RSPCA van seemed, at first, to be

impossible. He couldn't leap up into the kennel by himself, and Nick wasn't able to lift him without touching his skin and inflicting horrendous suffering. Eventually, Nick took the kennel out of the van and, with the rain sheeting down and his uniform soaked, he crouched down and spent about half an hour coaxing the petrified dog into the crate.

'He was pulling against me, and even doing that was causing him pain,' he remembers sadly. 'I couldn't scoop him up, as I normally would have done, because touching him was agony for him. There didn't seem to be anywhere on his body that wasn't ravaged. He was itching so badly that I don't think he would have been able to sleep, and that must have taken the spirit out of him.'

Finally in the van, the first stop for the pair was the local veterinary practice, run by vet Sonya and her husband. Everyone there was as shocked as the RSPCA officer had been at the sight of Eddie, who shuffled in behind Nick, his head bowed and his body language screaming, 'Enough!' The only voluntary movements he made were turning his head to try to pull the skin away from his body where the itching and pain were unbearable.

In over two decades working as a vet, Sonya had never seen a sight quite as tragic and distressing as that of Eddie, and she fervently hoped never to see a dog in such bad shape ever again. She had to choke back tears just remembering the first encounter with him: 'You get used to seeing a lot of nasty things as a vet, and you get quite hardened. But it was impossible to imagine the pain he was in. His distress was distressing for all of us to see. He was beyond whimpering, but he cried out in anguish if we tried to touch him, cowering away from people. He didn't know where to put his weight, as it exacerbated his pain just supporting himself.'

A massive 85 per cent of the surface area of Eddie's body was raw, weeping and infected. Sonya made the difficult decision that he was not beyond help, even though it remained to be seen whether he had enough resources to survive treatment and fight the infection. She decided to give it a go – he was worth all their efforts to keep him alive.

For the next hour and a half, she and her staff devoted themselves to gaining the defeated dog's trust enough for them to be able to put an anaesthetic line into him. As he passed gently into sleep, it must have been the first relief he had felt in months.

Then, for nearly two hours, Sonya and three members of the practice staff worked on poor old Eddie's devastated body, cutting away dead flesh and the remaining clumps of hair. Demodectic mites are invisible to the naked eye and can only be seen using a microscope, but just from the state of Eddie's skin Sonya knew without any further investigation that they were the culprits of his awful condition. The mites are parasites that live in hair follicles, and are one of three types of mites that can cause mange and fur loss in dogs. They're very common and most dogs have a natural immunity to them. Although they can never be completely eradicated, demodectic mites can be controlled and the problem contained if a vet treats the condition promptly.

When the initial work was complete, Eddie remained a sorry sight, with raw flesh wounds covering most of his body. Sonya administered a strong dose of analgesics, which gave him very much needed relief from his pain, and antibiotics to stop his wounds becoming infected.

That evening, as Eddie was slowly coming around from his anaesthetic, Kelly Snelling – the manager of The Lodge boarding kennels where Eddie would eventually spend much of his recovery time — was by coincidence collecting another dog from Sonya. When she saw the bloody, battered body of Eddie, she turned to Sonya in amazement.

'How can a dog look like that and still be alive?' she asked incredulously. As both Sonya and Nick had done, she wondered whether it might not have been kinder to have ended his suffering. 'He looks as if he's been skinned alive.'

Yet Sonya was hopeful: Eddie had survived the op and she could tell from his teeth, which she'd examined when he was under anaesthetic, that he was a young dog — between twelve and eighteen months old — which increased his chances of survival. Time was on his side. She told Kelly that her fingers were crossed, and she was feeling a lot more positive than when Eddie had first struggled in.

Her next challenge was finding a treatment to tackle the cause of his suffering, the mites. The standard treatment at that time was chemical baths, containing a strong organophosphate insecticide, but this was obviously not an option for a dog whose whole body was cracked, raw and open. The pain would have been unbearable for him, so it had to be something that could be given orally. Sonya consulted veterinary textbooks and research papers, and found a medicine that was licensed for the treatment of mites in farm animals. She decided that this was the best chance that Eddie had. To her great relief, the medication began to work straight away, and within twenty-four hours of arriving at the practice, Eddie showed encouraging signs of recovery.

It wasn't just his body, though — his improved appearance and physical strength — that gave all the practice staff heart. As soon as his pain was under control, it became evident his personality was friendly, warm and gentle. The life came back into him. For the first time, he wagged his tail, even though the flesh around it was clearly sore. He was eager to please and became a great favourite over the weeks that he stayed at the practice for treatment – which was covered by the practice's Waifs and Strays charity fund as well as by the RSPCA. The staff happily took it in turns to take him home at night for a bit of special attention.

For Sonya, the fact that Eddie's personality was so gentle and loving made it even harder for her to believe that anyone could have been so cruel to him, and she had to fight back her anger at whoever was responsible. Professionally, she remained calm and efficient, and focused her attention on helping Eddie regain his health, but it was hard to suppress her feelings of contempt and disgust towards the culprit.

While Eddie was receiving his treatment, Nick was investigating where Eddie had come from. He checked out the story from the man who'd found him at Christmas. The guy had supposedly rung the local dog wardens, but Nick discovered there was no such record of a phone call. As the man's home address was close to a local authority boundary, Nick even rang the wardens from two separate council areas to double-check. However, neither had heard about Eddie's plight, and they insisted they never would have refused to come out to a dog in need, even on Christmas Day. Nick also showed photos of Eddie to neighbours of the flat from where he had collected him, but nobody had seen the dog before.

Nick interviewed the man, suspecting there was more to his story, but when presented with the case file, the RSPCA prosecution department decided that there wasn't sufficient evidence to summons him to court. No further action was able to be taken. It's an all too common outcome and frustrating for all involved. Sometimes it's just not possible for inspectors to gather the evidence required for the RSPCA to be able to conduct a prosecution.

'His story of finding the dog may well have been true, but I was concerned about the days when he had him and must have been able to see he was in an excruciatingly painful condition. Surely he could see the dog needed professional care?' Nick recalls with evident frustration.

Three or four days after rescuing Eddie, Nick went back to see him at the veterinary practice. Although the dog was still a desperately sorry sight, with almost no fur left and his body covered in scabs and sores, Nick was thrilled at his transformation. He could see that Eddie's skin was starting to heal, and that his whole demeanour was different now he was no longer in dreadful pain. He wasn't scratching himself any more, he was happy to approach people, and his head, which had drooped before – indicating his crushed spirit – was now held up high, his large eyes taking everything in. From being a broken dog, who seemed to have given up on life and didn't want any human being near him, Eddie was now a friendly, trusting animal who sought out affection, and was happy to give it back in return. It was a remarkable turnaround in a very short space of time.

This rapid transformation confirmed to Sonya that she had made the right decision in giving Eddie's treatment a go. As his real shape began to emerge, the practice staff could see he looked like a German shepherd crossed with a husky, not the collie cross Sonya originally guessed he might be.

As soon as Eddie's open sores healed, which took almost a month, a programme of medicated baths was devised for him. By this point he was able to spend some of his time at The Lodge boarding kennels, a private local kennels used by the RSPCA, where manager Kelly Snelling, who had seen him at the vet's on the first night of his rescue and been horrified by his condition, was delighted to take on the role of Eddie's chief carer. She'd been in the job for fifteen years and was well used to the RSPCA bringing sad and uncared-for dogs to her, but she remembered Eddie's as the worst she'd ever come across; one that really stayed in her mind.

He came to The Lodge with a full treatment list: he had to be given antibiotics, ear drops, eye drops and the medicated baths. Kelly and her staff had never had to do so much for a dog, but he was so good natured they were more than happy to do it. What he didn't come with was a name. Although the staff at the vet practice had named him Eddie, this wasn't passed on to The Lodge, and, knowing he was a stray, Kelly and her staff decided to choose a name for him. To them, he became Jack, a confusion that means even to this day Nick and Kelly both refer to him as Eddie-Jack.

On his arrival at the kennels, Kelly was astonished that the miserable, desperate-looking animal she'd seen on his first night of treatment had turned out so well, and she was very thankful that vet Sonya had made the decision to give him a chance. She and her staff were amazed how happily he submitted to the constant rounds of treatment.

'When dogs have been in pain they can be forgiven for being a bit snappy when you have to administer treatments that they may not like, like eye drops and ear drops. But Eddie-Jack was never anything but wonderful. There was never a hint of aggression or even a sign that he didn't want you to do something. It was as if he understood it was all for his own good. He's a fabulous dog who won all our hearts,' she remembers with great fondness.

The news wasn't all good, however. When he first arrived at The Lodge, and for several weeks afterwards, Eddie exuded a particularly unpleasant smell, that of decaying tissue, which was being replaced by the new skin starting to cover his wounds. The antibacterial baths helped, but the staff who cared for him still remember the dreadful odour. It wasn't ideal but he certainly couldn't help it, and it didn't put any of them off their work with Eddie: his cheerful and gentle nature meant they all wanted to care for him in any way they could.

As his coat also started to recover, fur began to appear in small tufts all over his body, a look generously described by Sonya as 'inelegant — he was a bit of an ugly duckling for a while'.

For many days after his arrival at The Lodge, Eddie was ferried back to the veterinary practice on an almost daily basis for more treatment from Sonya. He spent his time at the practice making friends with everyone who visited, and the staff vied with each other to take him out for walks. Sonya would have loved to adopt him herself, but one of her own dogs was less than welcoming on the occasion Eddie stayed at their home.

That's why, about five months after Nick rescued him, once Eddie's condition improved, his wounds healed and fur began slowly to grow back, Sonya took the matter of re-homing him out of the hands of the RSPCA and put the story up on Facebook, complete with pictures of Eddie's transformation. His story touched people deeply, as she knew it would, and the pictures were shared thousands of times, with a deluge of applications coming in from people wanting to take Eddie on and give him the future he deserved. Some wanted to travel hundreds of miles to meet him.

One person who read his story was Laura Ellis, who, with her husband, Tom, and teenage son, Harvey, lived not far from Sonya's practice. Laura, who worked for the BBC, knew that Tom was really keen to have a dog. He'd always fancied a husky, but had been put off by stories of them not being good family pets and difficult to train. It was the suspected part-husky side of Eddie's background that made

Laura think Eddie could be the dog for Tom, and for the rest of the family.

She sent the Facebook link to Tom, who at the time was a stay-at-home dad to Harvey. He has treasured memories of his own pet dog, Grousie, named because the family got him on 12 August, the opening of the grouse season. He'd grown up with Grousie and had wanted a dog ever since starting his own family, but wasn't specifically looking for a new pet at the moment Eddie's story landed in his inbox. The sight of Eddie in recovery, however, filled his heart with grief at the poor dog's terrible history, admiration for the way the veterinary staff had pulled him through against the odds, and complete awe that a dog so badly injured possessed such a will to survive. Eddie was clearly a dog with character, and Tom felt he had to meet him. He booked an appointment to visit Sonya's practice the following day.

When Tom arrived, he came across a rather subdued Eddie — earlier that day the RSPCA had paid for him to be castrated, and he was still recovering from the anaesthetic. Nonetheless, the pair bonded immediately, with Eddie, who by this time had most of his fur back, licking Tom's hand enthusiastically, and Tom looking into his eyes and knowing that, if possible, he wanted Eddie in his life.

Sonya was immediately impressed by Tom's calm demeanour, and something told her that he and his family were the right choice to re-home the dog everyone at the practice had come to love. The staff were loath to give him up, but it was an inevitable part of the process and they were happy that they had made the right choice from all the applicants. A big bonus was that Tom lived near by, and would be able to bring Eddie back for any treatment he might need in the future.

Kennel manager Kelly, too, was delighted with the choice

of Tom and his family. She believed that Eddie was very lucky to have found them – but also that they are very lucky to have such a truly great dog.

'We've never had to work so hard on the treatment of any dog, but he was worth it all. We all fell in love with him – he's very special. His new owners are just the right people for him,' she said at the time.

When Tom got the good news that he'd been selected as Eddie's new owner, the whole family began to visit Eddie at The Lodge regularly, taking him out for walks around the local park. They discovered immediately that he was friendly, not just with people but with other dogs, too. It confirmed for Tom just how lucky they were to have found Eddie, who, in his words, is a 'tender, trusting, amazing dog who never stops giving'. Laura echoes his feelings, describing Eddie as a dog who just wants to please.

The first night in his new home, Tom followed advice from the kennels and put Eddie in a crate to sleep. Eddie was not happy, though, and that night he howled – a full, husky baying-at-the-moon howl. From then on he was never crated again – it simply wasn't the right thing for him and may have stirred up old memories. Instead, he settled very happily to sleep on his bed on the living-room floor. He's never howled again, and has slept soundly ever since; there haven't been any signs of troubled dreams in which he relives past suffering. Mercifully, he appears to have put all his pain and unhappiness firmly behind him.

When Eddie first moved in with Tom and Laura, some areas of his body were still bald and scarred, and it didn't seem likely that he would ever recover a full coat. The damage appeared to have been too great. Then, soon after he came home with the couple, there was a serious setback when he began to itch again. Tom, reacting quickly, took him back to Sonya, who shared his worries: sometimes demodectic mites recur throughout an animal's life. Eddie was given the same powerful medication that he'd had initially, and the outbreak cleared up very quickly. Thankfully, the mites have never come back again, and, against the odds, today Eddie has a thick, lustrous coat that attracts compliments wherever he goes.

The beauty of his new coat has surprised Sonya, who never thought it could be as special as it now is. She's pleased he has a complete covering of fur – he was so sad-looking without it – and it's a bonus to see it as full and luxuriant as it is. It took a full year for it to recover completely, which Sonya puts down to it needing a complete cycle of shedding and regrowth before they could see 'the real Eddie coat'.

The recurrence of Eddie's mite condition was, Tom believes, down to the stress of moving to new surroundings. In his short life, Eddie had at least one home before being rescued, then he was shuttled between the vet's and the kennels, settling happily into both. Being plucked from this familiarity, and a routine he'd grown used to, to then be taken to a new home by Tom and his family must have been disconcerting. He certainly didn't like going back on the medication, which he could taste in his food, but he had no choice other than to start taking it if he wanted a full tummy.

For months after his move to Tom and Laura's home, Eddie acted like a younger puppy. Dogs who haven't experienced a normal puppyhood will often revert to immature behaviour. He had to be taught to socialize off a lead with other dogs, but now he's very popular on the local dog-walking circuit. His distinctive looks make him a magnet for admiring comments, and his affectionate nature means he has his own fan club.

Not everyone in the house was entirely keen on Eddie's

arrival, however. Tom and Laura's three elderly cats kept a respectful distance, taking over the upstairs of the house and leaving Eddie to have the downstairs as his domain. Eddie has a natural fascination with small animals, chasing mice whenever he's on a walk through fields, and he's had to be trained not to chase sheep. So the cats made the right choice in giving him a wide berth, and Eddie has never encroached on their territory.

Almost three years down the line he's now very well trained, able to walk without a lead and observe a good road drill. Tom now has a full-time job, but he believes the fact that he had more time to put into training when Eddie first came home has paid dividends. He works just minutes away from the family home, however, and is still able to give Eddie four walks a day, including at lunchtime. Harvey and Laura still both dote on their new housemate, too.

'We all feel very blessed,' acknowledges Tom. 'We can't imagine life without him. I'd love to have seen him as a young puppy – he must have been beautiful before his skin condition took hold.'

Before he met Eddie, Tom had never considered owning a rescue dog, believing it was better to buy a puppy from a responsible breeder so that he would know its background, and be certain it was healthy and well bred – all things he felt he couldn't be sure about with a rescued dog of uncertain provenance.

'I couldn't have been more wrong,' he admits. 'All the things that put me off a rescued dog vanished from my mind the minute I met Eddie. His constitution is just right, his behaviour couldn't be better, and the amount of love and affection he gives is unrivalled. If we ever get another dog, we will definitely have a rescued one.'

Eddie's very happy to go back to the vet's whenever he

needs treatment or a routine check-up, and all the staff turn out to see him. He is, as Tom says, a 'bit of a star'. 'He trots off with the staff, and all you hear,' continues Tom, 'is different people saying, "Hello, Eddie."' They're all very fond of him because in all the time he spent there he was so well behaved and loving. 'He's a treasure, and everyone who knows him would agree.'

Eddie's case has had a significant impact on everyone who saw him in his terrible condition, none more so than Nick Wheelhouse, who has been an RSPCA inspector for more than seven years. Nick knows that in his job he makes a difference to animals' lives every single day, but it's cases such as Eddie's that stand out, because the difference between where the dog started at the point of rescue and where it ends up after being re-homed is so spectacular. Like Sonya, Nick had no idea that Eddie would transform into such a beautiful dog, or one with such a wonderful nature. At the beginning of Eddie's story, Nick wasn't sure he was going to make it at all.

'He's a completely different dog now, and that's a testimony to the hard work the vet and the family have put in. Seeing him now reinforces that what we do is 100 per cent worthwhile. When I was ushering that bedraggled, neglected, miserable dog into the kennel in the pouring rain, I couldn't have dreamt we would have this outcome. I really thought that perhaps the most charitable thing would be to put him out of his misery, and that he might not survive an operation, his body was in such poor shape. Thank God nobody gave up on him, and he didn't give up. His is a wonderful story.'

TIPS ON HOW TO CARE FOR YOUR DOG

Owners' responsibilities

DOG OWNERS have a legal responsibility under the Animal Welfare Act 2006 to protect their dog from pain, suffering, injury and disease. Checking your dog for signs of injury or illness every day, and making sure someone else does this if you are away, is the best way of ensuring that any health problems are spotted as early as possible, so they can be treated and managed. It's important that owners consult a vet promptly if they suspect that their dog is in pain, ill or injured, and only use medicines that have been prescribed for their individual dog. Signs that a dog may be ill or in pain include: decreased appetite and weight loss; drinking more or less water than normal; being unwilling to exercise or play; showing uncharacteristic fear or aggression when approached.

Take your dog for a routine health check with your vet at least once each year and ask your vet for advice about things you can do to protect your dog's health, such as vaccinations, neutering and treatments to control parasites (for example, fleas, mites and worms). Your vet can also give you advice about taking out pet insurance to ensure your dog is covered if they need veterinary treatment.

Dogs must wear a collar and tag when in a public place, and in April 2016 it became a legal requirement to have your dog microchipped in England and Wales. It applies to

▶

all dogs over the age of eight weeks and they need to be registered with an approved database such as Petlog (www.petlog.org.uk). As part of the new law, it's also a requirement for owners to keep their registered details up to date. This includes if you move house or change your telephone number.

CHAPTER 7

Poppy

IT WAS a worried member of the public who made the call, anonymously, to the RSPCA. There was a dog, the caller said, with half its fur missing, living in a house in Oxfordshire. They were disturbed by what they'd seen. Could the RSPCA do anything about it?

RSPCA Inspector Lauren Bailey covers Oxfordshire, so the call was referred to her. Heading to the property, she had no idea what she would find, or how bad it would be, but her guess was that the dog had fleas. Dogs can lose their fur from a nasty flea infestation, especially if they have an allergic reaction to flea bites. Lauren had seen it many times before.

It might just be a case of giving the owners some advice, she thought, showing them how to give flea treatment effectively, and simply letting them get on with it, armed with that all-important information. However, if the fur loss was severe, there might be no option but to take the dog away from its owner and get it some urgent veterinary treatment. In that scenario, the dog would be unlikely to be returned to its owner. It was Lauren's job to investigate.

She knocked on the door, explained why she was there, and the owner agreed to allow her in to see the dog. Lauren was over the first hurdle; her arrival isn't always welcome. Some owners become very defensive at the sight of an RSPCA officer on their doorstep. For others, aware that things have got out of control, it's a relief to know that someone is there to help.

The little Jack Russell, Poppy, was in an alarming state, even to the experienced eyes of an RSPCA officer who, over the years, has seen many animals with skin problems. Poppy's skin was scabby, inflamed and bleeding, and the poor animal was scratching incessantly, ripping open more tiny wounds all over her body in an attempt to find some relief. It didn't help that her claws were so long they were misshapen, and she was clearly underweight. The owner told Lauren she couldn't afford to take the little Jack Russell to a vet and, as Lauren asked more questions about the circumstances, it became clear that because of other worries, the owner had let Poppy slide to the bottom of her list of priorities. Lauren's intervention was not only needed, it was welcome.

Lauren explained carefully and clearly that Poppy needed to see a vet immediately, and the owner agreed to the RSPCA taking her for treatment. It was only when Lauren led the sad little dog out of the house into daylight that she could see clearly that as much as half of Poppy's fur was missing, and that the scabs were all over her body. Poppy trembled, her short, red-raw stub of a tail tucked firmly between her legs, as she timidly followed Lauren outside. On the doorstep, as she was leaving, Lauren had to issue a caution to the owner.

'Because she hasn't been taken to a vet, and her condition has clearly been going on for such a long time, and because she's potentially suffering, there may have been offences committed,' she warned.

It's dependent on the professional opinion of a vet as to whether or not an animal is suffering, even when it's obviously the case, as it was for poor Poppy. It has to be an expert veterinary opinion and Lauren isn't qualified to give that, though it didn't take a medically trained eye to see that the little dog was in a lot of pain and very unwell. Lauren was very worried for her well-being, and felt sure that any vet who examined Poppy would also be deeply concerned about her.

Lauren was anxious about lifting Poppy into her van because of the discomfort she was in. She was so fragile, small and vulnerable. Lauren put a blanket down in the cage, aware that the last thing Poppy needed was to be on a hard plastic floor. She wanted her to be as comfortable as possible because she knew that any undue pressure on Poppy's already fragile flesh would be unbearable for the little dog.

Lauren drove her precious charge to West Bar Veterinary Hospital, where vet James Carrier lifted Poppy very gently on to his examination table. He quickly agreed that she had a very severe skin condition. There were bald patches on her face, but the main areas affected were down her back and around her tail, which was docked. As Lauren had observed, her claws were very overgrown.

As he was examining Poppy, James spotted a live flea that had fallen from her body on to the table, and he could see others crawling on her remaining tufts of fur. An infestation has to be particularly bad for fleas to be seen so obviously. However, to James it was clear that fleas were only part of

Poppy's problem. He continued to look through her fur for other live parasites — ticks and mites that are picked up by dogs from long grass and tall plants. As he suspected, she had a severe parasite infestation, which was identified by a skin scrape. One of her ears was very tender and painful, and was filled with a waxy pus — an infection which had set in as a result of her lowered immune system.

'It's a really severe infestation, all down to her generally poor condition. She's very sore,' he told Lauren.

Poppy didn't object to being looked at, but every so often she gave a tiny whimper, which reminded James and Lauren that she was in distress. When Lauren asked James to assess officially how poorly Poppy was, James explained that an animal's body weight and condition is often graded on a scale from one to nine, with a nine being a dog in fantastic shape. It's a subjective assessment, but in his opinion Poppy was close to a two. It doesn't get much worse than the state Poppy was in.

Lauren, by this time, was completely invested in Poppy's well-being and was nervous for her. 'What can you do? Will she recover? Can she ever be a normal dog again?' she asked James.

It would take a long time for her skin to recover, he explained, and even longer for her fur to grow back. It was the worst case he'd seen of a skin condition like this. The medical plan was to start by doing blood tests to show if she had any underlying problems, and to give her some antibiotics and anti-parasite drugs to stop the infernal itching as quickly as possible.

Lauren had to ask her crucial questions: 'Is she suffering? Should her owner have done more?'

James was unequivocal. 'A reasonable owner would have taken Poppy to a vet and not let her get into this state,' he declared. It was a damning but necessary conclusion, and the confirmation from a medical professional that Lauren needed in order to take action.

Lauren left the poor little dog in the excellent hands of James and the experienced team at his practice and went back to see the owner. This time, she invited the owner to officially sign Poppy over to the RSPCA. The owner agreed. She'd neglected Poppy's health because of her stressful family problem, and it was deemed that a formal caution would be appropriate in the circumstances. Lauren was sympathetic to the family's circumstances, so she issued it and took no further action. From here on, the priority was restoring Poppy to full health, finding her a new home and putting this terrible chapter in her short life behind her.

After life-saving treatment for Poppy was initiated at West Bar Veterinary Hospital, she was then transferred to the RSPCA animal centre in Oxford to be looked after until she was fit enough to be re-homed. A full programme of treatment was prescribed, including daily medicated baths, drops for her ears, and a lotion for her sore and itchy skin.

Poor little Poppy's problems weren't simply physical, though. Her prolonged neglect had also left deep psychological scars. In addition to her skin woes, for which she was at last receiving good medical care, she was also terribly sad and unhappy. The staff and volunteers at the animal centre were very worried about her. By comparison, her obvious physical problems seemed very manageable; but she was so low in spirits, so lacklustre and cowed, that they could see she needed more tender loving care than living in the shelter could provide. She needed more than simply being with other recovering animals and being tended to by committed staff.

That was when volunteer Linda Oliver had a good idea:

what Poppy needed was a foster home, with loving carers who would look after her around the clock and give her the affection she craved, until she was back to full health. A huge dose of love was prescribed as part of Poppy's healing process.

Linda thought she knew just the right people for the job: her sister-in-law, Fay Joines, and Fay's husband, Jim. The problem was that Fay and Jim weren't looking for a dog. However, Linda's plea to them was heartfelt – she knew that if Poppy was to thrive and not merely survive, then she needed to be cared for in a really special way. When she described to Fay and Jim how desperate the little dog was, how miserable she was even at the RSPCA centre where she was well cared for, they found it impossible to say no.

'Linda said that Poppy wouldn't be any problem, but that she needed help, that living in a kennel was bad for her,' Fay recalls. 'It broke my heart imagining it, so we agreed to take her on a temporary basis. We were told that even then she only had a fifty-fifty chance of pulling through.'

The couple was reluctant to take on a dog because their own dog, Jasper, whom they'd had for twelve years, had died three years earlier. Jasper was a border collie crossed with a springer spaniel and they'd had him since he was a puppy. His death had distressed Fay so much that she'd come close to having a breakdown. She'd been devastated, and the loss had been so overwhelming that she'd had to take time off work.

They'd then fostered a dog for Linda quite soon after Jasper died, a Cavalier King Charles spaniel called Cookie. When Cookie came along, Jim was afraid that Fay would get too attached, and Fay did indeed fall in love with her. Parting with Cookie after three months, when she was finally permanently re-homed, had been difficult for Fay. She would have kept her if it had been possible. Cookie's departure had brought back the struggle Fay had had after Jasper died and she kept in touch with Cookie's new owner for about a year in order to soften the blow and weather the transition period. That's when she and Jim agreed: 'No more dogs.'

With all this in mind, Jim was anxious to spare Fay any more emotional stress when the call came about Poppy. It was no surprise that Jim was initially uncertain about taking her. He eventually backed down, though, so Linda brought Poppy round to their home in Kidlington, near Oxford, to introduce her.

It was a winning move. As soon as Fay and Jim saw Poppy, they knew they had to give her all the help they could. She was in a desperately sad state. She had no hair down her back or sides, there was fur only on one side of her head, and her tail was so red-raw that she couldn't sit down. She looked pitiful and, at first, she was so sore all over that it was impossible to stroke or cuddle her without causing her pain. They had to fight their instincts to smother her with affection and wait for her to heal and be ready to be touched.

'The day she first sat on my lap, I cried with happiness,' Fay remembers. 'We'd taken her to the allotment, and while Jim was digging I was sitting on the bench. She came to me and climbed on to my lap, and it was the best feeling in the world.'

When Poppy first arrived, her medical treatment was in full swing. She had to be given a medicated bath every day, with a special shampoo provided by the RSPCA, and her sore skin had to be coated with soothing lotion. Omega oil also had to be added to her food to promote the regrowth of her fur. She was happy to let Fay pick her up to treat her, and would look at her as if to say, 'Help me.' However, Fay could see that even the gentlest handling hurt her.

Lauren, the inspector who rescued Poppy initially, visited her a few weeks into her treatment and immediately could see she was a different little dog from the fragile, timid, miserable one she rescued. She'd put on weight, was happy, bright and confident. Even though her fur hadn't grown back much, the immediate transformation was amazing. Just not being in permanent pain had done so much for her.

Poppy had lived with Fay and Jim for about three months before she first wagged her tail, partly because it took her that long to feel secure and happy, but also because her scabby, furless, docked tail was clearly still very painful. In those early weeks and months, Jim spent a lot of time sitting with her, quietly, until she felt safe with him. She nipped a little at first, and Jim was usually on the receiving end of that. It was perhaps a residual memory, Jim felt. Perhaps he reminded her of someone in her past. He remained patient, though, and would put his hand down and let her sniff it, so that she could see he wasn't going to hurt her.

It took about six months for Poppy to stop clawing at her itchy, painful skin, but gradually the scratching abated. Also, at the same time as the itching was easing, Poppy's weight was slowly coming back up to normal, as the couple carefully increased her food incrementally, as advised. Poppy was beginning to look well.

Lauren, who has been an inspector for more than five years, says skin conditions are one of the most common problems she sees. 'Poppy's skin was horrendous, but sadly I've seen many cases just as bad. What's really tragic is that it's one of the easiest things to deal with if it's treated early. Yet when it's left to get out of hand, it can be so painful and debilitating for the dog.'

Initially it was very difficult to get Poppy to settle at night. Fay and Jim borrowed a crate from Linda, and sleeping inside it seemed to make the little dog feel more secure. Fay changed the bedding every day, because Poppy was shedding so many flakes of skin. After a couple of weeks in the security of her new and loving home, she decided she didn't need to go in the crate any more, and has slept upstairs with her beloved owners ever since.

Sometimes she would bed down inside the fitted wardrobe, but then, in the middle of the night, would come to one side of the bed. It was too high for her to leap on to, so either Fay or Jim would lift her up. And she loved it. The warmth and proximity to her loving carers make for a good night's sleep. She goes right under the duvet, burrowing deep to find the most comfy spot, probably because having so little fur means that she feels the cold, Fay suggests. When the little pup is downstairs she loves to sit on Jim's shoulder, licking his ears. He's her go-to buddy then, but in bed it's Fay she snuggles up with.

From the beginning, Poppy's behaviour, as Linda had assured them, was good – she was quiet and timid, and Jim and Fay's greatest challenge was to help restore her spirit – but it took time to house-train her, and Fay and Jim were constantly cleaning up after her for the first few weeks. She got the hang of it in time, and now she stands by the door when she needs to go out.

She's odd about doors, though, and even if a door is ajar, she won't push it open herself, but will stand and wait for someone to do it for her. Fay wonders if in the past she got into trouble for going into rooms she wasn't supposed to be in. She and Jim will never know for sure what Poppy went through with her previous owner – they weren't given any details of her past life and believe that's the right decision. They don't want to know who neglected her; they don't want to think about it. In their eyes, it's beyond belief that anyone could let a little dog get in that state.

However, it was only when they first tried to take her out for a walk that the couple realized that Poppy had never been outside. She was terrified of everything she saw. She would turn and try to go back into the house, and if she was on a lead she would plant herself and simply refuse to move from the doorstep.

It was a steep learning curve for them all; a slow and gradual process. It was clear Poppy had never even seen a cat before either, and she knew nothing about roads or traffic, so Fay and Jim were petrified of letting her off the lead. She seemed never to have walked on grass. Even the smallest noise petrified her.

At first, they started off with little walks, just around the local area, to get her used to being outside, and rewarded her with lots of treats. After a few months, Poppy graduated to going to the park, where she's happy to socialize with other dogs and loves madly chasing a ball, even if she hasn't yet got the hang of bringing it back to Jim. They also take her to some nearby fields, where she runs exuberantly – as if she hasn't a care in the world. It's taken a couple of years but getting her to that point is a huge success story.

'We used a very long lead at first, to teach her to come back to us, and rewarded her when she did it,' explains Jim. 'She's a bright little dog and she got the hang of it very quickly. She had clearly had no training at all before she came to us. She thinks everyone is her friend and rushes up to play with them. That's her natural personality coming through. Whatever happened to her in those early months and years hasn't damaged the kind, gentle, lovely girl that she is.'

During Poppy's first winter with Jim and Fay, she wore a small, knitted yellow coat, made for her by Fay, who was worried about her getting cold without any fur. She was also supposed to be fully grown, but was still terribly thin and small. Fay bought her a waterproof coat, too, and for two winters she was happy to be dressed for trips outside.

However, as her fur started to recover, she made it clear that she wasn't happy wearing a coat any more. She's a much bigger dog now, and far more robust, so although they've bought her bigger coats, she now refuses to wear them. Even though her fur still isn't yet back to normal, she can do a much better job of retaining her own body heat.

Fay knew as soon as Poppy moved in with them that she wanted to keep her, but Jim and Linda urged caution because they were aware how difficult it would be for Fay if Poppy didn't pull through, or if she had to be re-homed elsewhere for other reasons. As soon as it was clear that Poppy was pulling through all her health problems, Fay and Jim formally adopted her, six weeks after she moved in with them.

'I promised them I wouldn't get so attached this time, but it's not easy, and I was already besotted with her within days,' says Fay. 'She's such a character. Even in her pain she was a loving little dog.'

Both Jim and Fay grew up with dogs, and they love the presence of a furry friend around the house. They acquired Jasper when the youngest of their five children, Dougie, was six years old, and had been pestering them to get a dog. It was his older brother, Darren, a teenager at the time, who shared the care of Jasper with Fay and Jim, and who had Jasper on his bed every night. Now all the Joines children and their six grandchildren dote on Poppy, who has never been so well loved.

When Poppy was first taken in by the RSPCA, the guess was that she was about seven years old. However, as soon as she began to recover physically, it was clear that she was much younger. Now, Fay and Jim, and the vet, think she was about two and a half when she came to them.

Two years since she moved in, Poppy's fur is growing back, but is still very thin and patchy in places. On the side of her head, which was once completely bald, she now has a fuzz of new hair. The red blotches still appear occasionally, but, unlike her previous owner, Jim and Fay are vigilant about looking for them and acting quickly when there's an outbreak.

The healing process has been slow but she's improving all the time. However, Poppy's nasty ear infection may have left its mark: Fay and Jim suspect she is partially deaf because, even after having her ears cleaned out by the vet, she seems to have some residual hearing loss. She also has a very sensitive stomach, possibly the result of being underfed and then having so many antibiotics to treat her infections. She's had one severe episode of sickness and, despite tests and X-rays, there was no explanation for it, so Fay and Jim just make sure to feed her carefully — two small meals a day with an expensive health food, and very few treats. Her one gastronomic luxury comes if Fay cooks a roast dinner at the weekend, and Poppy gets a small piece of plain chicken.

Looking back, Jim and Fay know for certain that they made the right decision to help the RSPCA out with Poppy. 'It wasn't us who were doing them a favour — they were doing us a favour. Poppy is one of the best things that has happened to us. We really love having her. She's so funny, kind, lovely. We feel very lucky to have her,' says Fay. 'It's lovely to think of Poppy having such a happy life now.'

TIPS ON HOW TO CARE FOR YOUR DOG

Health conditions

SKIN PROBLEMS are a common issue in dogs and can have many different triggers: fleas, for example, and even certain foods. Signs that a dog might have an allergic skin condition include excessive scratching and soreness. If owners are worried their dog may be affected, they should seek advice from a vet, who will be able to provide advice tailored to the individual dog.

Some breeds and types of dogs are particularly prone to inherited disorders and diseases. Before deciding to get a dog, it's important to find out what health and behaviour problems they might have, or may be prone to as a result of their breed, as well as how they've been bred and how they've been cared for.

Some breeds of dog have also been selected for exaggerated physical features, such as a short flat face, heavy wrinkles and a very long back. Sadly, although these features may be considered 'normal' for a breed, they can cause dogs to suffer and reduce their quality of life. For example, dogs with short flat faces often have narrow nostrils and tiny windpipes. They can be affected by severe breathing difficulties and may even struggle to enjoy a walk or playing. Folded or wrinkled skin may be itchy and painful, and infolding eyelids can scratch a dog's eyeball.

▶

Some of these problems will require lifelong medication or sometimes surgery.

Vets can provide help and advice for owners who are unsure if their dog may have a breed-related health issue, or for people who are interested in getting a dog but would like to know more about the different problems that certain breeds may be susceptible to.

CHAPTER 8

William

NEITHER RACHEL nor Chris can imagine life without William now. He is happiest lying on the sofa next to his new owners, his head resting on a knee, looking up with the big dark eyes that first struck such a deep chord with Rachel. But now the eyes are not pleading for help. They are happy eyes, full of energy and light.

Rachel marvels at how William has been able to put his early treatment behind him and become the sprightly little pup he was clearly always going to be. He's come such a long way in such a short space of time that it's hard for anyone who meets him today to appreciate just how close to death he was when he first came into their lives.

It began with Inspector Nicky Foster walking into the RSPCA Coventry Animal Centre for a routine visit and seeing two people standing at the reception desk, one of them holding a small dog wrapped in a blanket. Nicky, who has been an RSPCA inspector for more than twelve years, will never forget the shock she felt on first seeing the emaciated puppy. Even through the blanket she could make out his skeletal frame. There was no flesh on his face and not even enough muscle tone in his neck to support his head. It was clear, even at a glance, that he was in a very bad way, barely clinging to life.

The couple claimed they'd found him by the side of the road and, after trying to look after him for a day or two – in which time they could see he was getting worse – had decided to bring him to the centre. Nicky took down their details but her main concern was the little dog, who was in desperate need of emergency care. She took him into her arms and was horrified to feel through the blanket just how skinny he was – he barely weighed anything. Carefully, she carried him to her van and whisked him away to vet Molly Crawley, who was just as horrified as Nicky at the state of the pitiful bundle of bones.

The puppy was immediately put on an intravenous drip to get his fluid levels up, and re-feeding was gradually started. The veterinary staff began by giving him very small amounts of food at regular intervals, so that his digestive system became accustomed to working again. He remained so weak he was unable to stand, and had to be given a heat mat to lie on – with so little flesh it was difficult for him to maintain his body temperature. He weighed just 3kg, about a third of the weight he should have been, and less than the average weight of a newborn baby. On a body condition score out of five, the vet rated him as zero.

Being a stray, he had no name, and Nicky initially decided to call him Harry, after her son, whose second birthday it was on the day the puppy was brought in. However, she soon realized that the little pup didn't look like a Harry, so she opted for her son's middle name, William, instead. Thanks to William, or Skinny William as everyone who knew him in the early days after his rescue called him, Nicky was late home on Harry's birthday, but she knew that the delay was for a worthy cause.

'In this job, not many cases really get to you, but this little chap definitely did. I had to remain professional, of course, but my heart went out to this scrawny scrap of a puppy, who was probably only hours away from death,' she recalls with great sadness.

William, who appeared to be some kind of greyhound but whose pedigree was uncertain, was in a critical condition. For the first twenty-four hours under the vet's care, it was really touch and go as to whether he'd survive. He lay list-lessly on his heat mat, without either the energy or will even to turn himself over. The staff at the vet's moved him regularly, to prevent more pressure sores from developing. Caused by his inability to change position, William's poor, ravaged body was already covered in them. It was clear he'd been in a state for quite some time.

The wonderful, dedicated staff at the practice continued to look after William and three days later, when Nicky saw him again, she couldn't believe the effect such a short period of good care had had on William's health. Not only had he survived, but he was also off the drip and eating enthusiastically. The team at the veterinary practice had established that he was putting on weight well, so there was no medical reason for his emaciated condition other than a basic lack of food and nutrition. Put simply, little William had been starving to death, and had been rescued in the nick of time.

Yet despite all the good news, his muscles had atrophied and there was still a risk that his liver and kidneys had been damaged. It would be a couple of weeks before further blood tests would reveal any serious or ongoing health problems. On top of this, even after three days of food, and an opportunity to regain his strength in a controlled environment, William could still only support his own weight for two or three seconds. However, he was much brighter and more alert than when she first saw him, so Nicky took him to stay with an experienced RSPCA foster carer for the second phase of his care.

As the veterinary nurses had done, the carer too had to continue to physically move him in order to relieve the pressure on his existing sores and prevent more from developing. She also had to carry him outside to let him poo and wee, but he was gradually struggling to get up under his own steam and, most importantly, he was showing signs of wanting to survive. The crushed and beaten little animal that Nicky had first carried into the vet's was being replaced by a sparky little chap who was taking notice of what was going on around him.

A couple of weeks later, when Nicky picked William up to take him back to see the vet, she was even more thrilled to see how much he had improved. Molly's face also lit up at the transformation of her sickly patient as he walked in unaided, tail wagging, and expressing an interest in sniffing her hand. Nicky was able to report that William was holding food down, there had been no vomiting or diarrhoea, and Molly in turn was able to tell Nicky that she thought William was about six months old — he'd been so poorly when she first saw him that even a wild estimation of his age had been impossible.

The little pup was still very fragile and hadn't yet built up any muscle, so could only walk for short periods, but every day he was getting stronger. His right front leg seemed to be weaker than his other legs, but he wasn't in any pain, and Molly didn't think it was because of any underlying damage. With time, she hoped it would heal.

'He first came in looking like a skeleton,' said Molly. 'Now he's skinny but he's starting to look like a proper little dog. He's still significantly underweight, but he's on his way.'

New blood tests revealed that the serious anaemia from which William had been suffering was now much better and showed, Molly explained, in the pinkness of his gums. She was also able to rule out liver and kidney damage. The news was much like winning the lottery for the puppy — he was very lucky to have escaped long-term and more serious health problems.

Nicky was elated, because she'd honestly not been expecting him to survive, let alone make such a promising recovery. 'He's a very lucky little puppy. When I first saw him I wasn't hopeful that we would ever see this day.'

While the foster carer carefully continued to bring William's weight up, Nicky faced another challenge: tracing the owners who had allowed this vulnerable dog to get into the state he was found in. She'd taken photographs of his awful condition when she first saw him, and now she made a call to the RSPCA's press officer for the area, Rachel Butler, suggesting they needed a press appeal to see if anyone could give them any information about him. She forwarded the photographs to Rachel, so she could see William for herself.

'As soon as I opened the file of pictures on my computer I

was struck by William's eyes,' remembers Rachel. 'He looked so sad and helpless, but there was a look that seemed to be appealing for help.'

Rachel's press release struck a nerve with both local and national newspaper journalists. The harrowing pictures of skeletal William appeared on the front page of the *Coventry Telegraph*, and across the national press, including the *Daily Mail* and the *Mirror*, as well as on social media. The response from the public was immediate and large, many of the readers just expressing their enormous outrage and sadness that anyone could allow a little dog to be reduced to this state, but others giving useful information about the puppy's owners.

'Quite a few people told us who they believed the owners were,' said Nicky. 'It was the couple who had brought him in. I'd accepted their story at the time because it seemed plausible, but it was now clear they'd made it up. I went round to their home with a colleague, and when they opened the door they said, "We were expecting you." The sheer volume of outrage about the little dog had made them aware we would find out who they were.'

Nicky was surprised that the couple hadn't been able to cope with the puppy. They had children, a cat and another dog, all of whom were well fed and cared for. Apparently, they'd fancied having a puppy, seen him advertised, and simply bought him. It was clear to Nicky that they hadn't researched what a puppy needs to thrive. They need a great deal of care, and the couple had bought William on a whim, without any idea how to look after him. They'd been feeding him far too little and not often enough – they hadn't read up that puppies need small meals regularly. When he could no longer get out of his bed to defecate but did it where he lay, they took him in to the centre.

It was impossible for Nicky to understand how they could not have seen, just by looking at him, that William needed more food. What was going through their minds? Denial about his worsening condition? Shame about their failure to act in time? As his health deteriorated it was appalling neglect not to take him to a vet to get some expert advice and some basic medical attention.

Everyone who saw William when he first came into the RSPCA centre could tell that the state he was in hadn't developed overnight. It defies belief that it wasn't apparent to his owners that he was literally starving to death, and Nicky was horrified and heartbroken that they'd let him get to the verge of dying before seeking help.

Among the people who came forward after the publicity about William was the breeder who had sold him as a puppy. Nicky and her colleague paid him a visit and, during the course of the interview, completely exonerated him of any wrongdoing. The puppy was healthy when he was sold, and because the couple were experienced dog owners, there was no reason for the breeder to suspect they would neglect and starve him. He, too, couldn't understand how they let it happen.

Poignantly for Nicky, the breeder still owned William's sister, and the comparison between the two dogs was heartrending. His sister was a normal, healthy dog of a good weight, a living illustration of how William should look.

William's previous owners were successfully prosecuted and given a suspended prison sentence, fined and banned from keeping animals for life. Their other pets were re-homed through their friends and family. For once, it was a very satisfactory outcome for those wanting justice for William.

Nicky discovered that the little puppy was a greyhound-saluki cross, and although his original owners had named him George, she decided that William, the name she had given him, suited him better. It was good for him to have a new name for his new, happier life and she continued to see him regularly on his road to recovery, whenever his foster carer brought him into the animal centre with her, where she worked.

'I watched him turn around. He was so young, still growing in height, so every time I saw him he was transformed. It only took a few weeks for it to be unbelievable he had ever been so thin and in such a dispirited state,' she said.

Nicky wasn't the only one who was monitoring William's recovery. Despite dealing with RSPCA stories of the ill treatment of animals every day, Rachel Butler, the press officer who first told the world about the sad little puppy, was particularly moved by William, and found she couldn't stop thinking about him.

She and her partner, Chris, already had an elderly Westie called Harry, but they'd wanted another dog for a long time. When she first saw the shocking pictures of William, Rachel had told Chris all about him, and pulled the images up on the computer to show him.

'Chris loves animals as much as I do. I'd only been in my job for eight weeks at that time, and Chris and I hadn't planned to take on another dog just then. But I couldn't get this emaciated little dog out of my mind. I kept in touch with Nicky to check on his progress, and one day she told me that William was beginning to show playful tendencies, more like a puppy. That was when I decided I had to meet him,' Rachel remembers.

The following day she drove to the Coventry Animal Centre, taking with her toys and dog biscuits for William. She hadn't mentioned to Chris that she was going. In her heart, she was hoping to adopt the puppy, but she knew it might not be a straightforward process.

It was about four weeks after his rescue that Rachel first met William, and he was still very thin. He was in the office at the animal centre with his foster carer, running around, really playful, ingratiating himself with everyone who came in. He was wearing a cute jumper because he felt the cold, but his personality was shining through. Despite what he'd been through, it was immediately obvious to Rachel that he was a very happy, carefree puppy, who loved to create mayhem.

Even though he wasn't yet house-trained it didn't put her off, but she didn't want to tell the staff at the centre that she wanted to become William's new owner. She was sure that, after so much publicity, there would be a queue of people wanting to adopt him, and there was the possibility that she wouldn't be selected as the best candidate. However, on her way home all she could think was, 'I really, really want him.'

A couple of days later she told Chris. They'd originally planned to have another small dog, as she was used to dogs of Harry's size, but Chris had always liked greyhounds. By this time, Rachel had mentioned to the manager of the centre that she was keen to have William, and, as she feared, the centre had been bombarded with offers to adopt him. However, because Rachel worked from home for the RSPCA, she was put to the top of the list of potential owners. She was in with a shot, and for the first time she allowed herself to feel properly excited.

Rachel and Chris agreed they would take Harry to the centre to meet William, to see if they hit it off. If there was any animosity between them, any friction at all, then Rachel's dream would be over. There's a ten-year age gap between the two dogs, and she and Chris wanted to be absolutely sure that Harry would be happy with the new addition to the family. They took the two dogs for a walk together to test out the dynamic.

'William was such a clown, lolloping around on his long, gangly legs, wrapping his lead around Chris. That was the moment that Chris fell in love with him, and was as convinced as I was that William belonged with us. William made him laugh, and Chris said there and then that he wanted him,' Rachel recalled.

'He was really funny,' Chris agreed. 'He was tripping over his own legs. He made me laugh, and he still makes me laugh all the time.'

The couple paid the adoption fee, but as they were in the process of moving house at the time, it was agreed that William would stay at the centre for a little longer, rather than having him disrupted by the experience of two different houses in a matter of weeks. The staff at the centre were desperately sad to see him moving on, as he'd worked his way into all their affections during his stay.

When re-homing day finally came, on the journey home Rachel held the whimpering little dog on her lap in the back seat of the car, trying to comfort him. He had no idea what was happening to him, or where he was going. Her sister met them outside the house with Harry, as they'd been advised to reintroduce the pair away from the house, which was very much Harry's territory. As soon as he saw the little Westie, William jumped from the back seat of the car to the front seat, so excited was he to see his new doggy pal.

Harry, on the other hand, was a bit bemused. He'd never lived with another dog, and in those first few weeks wasn't entirely welcoming to the newcomer, getting up and walking away if William tried to settle down next to him. Despite the slightly rocky start, they've since become great companions, and William's lively presence seems to have rejuvenated Harry, who's found his playful side again.

Rachel took a few days off work to help William settle,

and it turned out that she really needed it. It was a stressful time, with William crying all through the first night and no one getting much sleep. She also discovered how much more work goes into walking a lively, strong dog than an elderly Westie, and that new carpets and a dog with a sensitive stomach and no house-training do not really go together . . . Because he'd been starved, William's digestive system remained very delicate, and it took a while for Rachel and Chris to find the right, balanced diet for him.

At the time, the problems felt considerable. William also suffered from extreme separation anxiety. His short life had been so chequered – from being starved, to staying at the vet's, to living with the foster carer, to being in kennels at the animal centre, to eventually being at home with his new owners – he didn't know what to make of it all. Even if Rachel and Chris were upstairs for only five minutes, William would become very distressed, crying and defecating through worry. He destroyed everything he could find.

Rachel and Chris knew they had to cope with it all, understanding that his behaviour was a result of the terrible time he'd had, and that he simply needed time, patience and a lot of love to settle. Rachel set up a remote camera, and they could see that when she and Chris weren't there, William would whimper, cry and pace around the house. An animal behaviourist paid them a visit to give them advice, and they started a programme of incremental leaving – at first just for five minutes, gradually longer. They were taught not to make a fuss of him when they left or when they got back, which felt alien to them, as they'd always fussed with Harry when they returned from leaving him alone. William was a very different personality, though, with a set of complicated psychological issues that presented a considerable challenge.

It took more than a year before William had calmed down enough for the couple to leave him for three or four hours with Harry for company, and without Harry he is OK for just a couple of hours on his own. Harry spends weekends with Rachel's sister, as he was their family dog originally, so William had to be taught to cope without him. Those couple of hours mean she and Chris can go to the supermarket alone, or even pop out to eat. While that's a huge step forwards, there's still some way to go. The impact on the couple's lifestyle has been huge.

Despite his anxiety about being on his own and his other behavioural problems, within a few days of arriving home with Rachel and Chris, William's natural personality started to emerge.

'He's friendly, bouncy, mischievous, lively, always trying to steal my slippers,' reveals Rachel.

William's stomach continues to be sensitive, and Rachel once took him to the vet when he refused to eat breakfast in the morning, worried about the possible danger of him missing out on nutrition after his miraculous recovery. However, it turns out that William is a lazybones who loves a lie-in. He's happy to eat breakfast later, but he doesn't want it the minute he wakes up, especially if he's been out for a long walk the day before, when he'll happily stay in his bed until ten o'clock.

Although he likes a late breakfast, he's still very possessive about his food and has to be fed separately from Harry, who has learned not to go near William's bowl. He also used to hide dog chews around the house – squirrelling them away just in case there might not be any more coming his way, Rachel thought. In the early days in his new home, he tried to drink from the toilet, and Rachel wonders if he'd been forced to find water that way in his original home. He licks the dew off plants in the garden and when they're out for walks, another sign that he had been dehydrated in his early days and had learned how to make the most of any water around.

His legs still bear the scars from the numerous pressure sores he endured, and there's a hole which goes right through one of his ears. Chris and Rachel have no real idea what his previous home was like, but they were wary of introducing him to children initially. They knew he'd been living with two in his first, unhappy home and that there was the possibility other children might trigger unhappy memories.

'But we were wrong to worry, as he's brilliant with them. My cousin's three-year-old, Finley, loves William and William loves him. In fact, William seems to be less boisterous when Finley is around,' Rachel says. It's as if he understands that children might not respond well to excitable behaviour.

His dew claws are missing, and Rachel wonders if they were removed so that he could be used for hare coursing, which is what greyhound-saluki crosses are often bred for. Dew claws can cause problems such as sores if they get ripped while coursing, and so the easiest thing is to get rid of them. When he first came home he hated having his paws touched by anyone, and he panicked if Rachel or Chris went near them. Now that he accepts his new owners completely, they can handle him without any fuss.

For Rachel and Chris, William is like a puzzle they're trying to solve. By observing his behaviours, they're beginning to make sense not only of who he is now, but of who he used to be. He is sociable with other dogs that he meets, especially if he is off his lead, and if they are smaller than him. He remains cautious about men, however, especially when he meets them for the first time, and he's naturally protective of Rachel, walking near her whenever a man he doesn't recognize approaches – he doesn't behave like that when he's being walked by Chris. Rachel works from home most of the time, but when she has to go out for the day, her uncle is a willing dogsitter, and William is glad of the company. Now that he has calmed down, William is not a demanding charge.

By the time William was adopted, the RSPCA had made sure he was castrated and also microchipped. However, because he's capable of running at great speed, Rachel and Chris only ever let him off the lead when they're in an enclosed place, not in woods or open country where he could be miles away before becoming tired enough to slow down. Chris is a runner, but even he wouldn't stand a chance of keeping up with a dog that has been bred for speed. Although they're training him to have a better recall, and he's improving, he's not yet completely reliable. He's been with the family for over two years now, but it's still necessary to keep a close eye on him. They wouldn't want to lose him.

After his initial reservations about a new dog, Harry has completely accepted William, and they are now happiest curling up together on the sofa, with Harry gently licking William's nose from time to time. William's laziness doesn't stop with refusing to get out of bed early – he also likes to sleep all day in the sunroom. Like all dog breeds with thin coats, he loves warmth, and if he joins Chris and Rachel in the bedroom, he burrows right under the duvet. He's incredibly content.

The prosecution of William's original owners took place the week that the puppy moved in with Rachel and Chris, and Rachel felt particularly pleased that by the time they came before the court William was already in his new home, settling down to a new life.

'It seemed significant. They had signed him over to the RSPCA, so we were free to adopt him before the case started, and I wanted him home with us, symbolically, at the start of his official new life. As the press officer involved in the case I went to court to see them sentenced. I wanted to look at the people who had done this to him. It was weird being there. I felt angry just being in the same room as them. I was there professionally, so didn't show my feelings.'

Though it was a difficult time, the court case helped Rachel and Chris draw a line under William's past problems, giving him the new start he deserved.

Rachel and Chris had just become engaged when they adopted William. Ten months after he moved in with them, he had a starring role on their wedding day. The couple wanted both Harry and William at the ceremony, and when they were looking at venues the first question Rachel asked at prospective locations was whether they could have dogs at the ceremony.

'Lots of places said we could have them outside for pictures, but we wanted them to play a part. William was a pageboy and Harry was the ring bearer. William is much bouncier than Harry and we didn't want to risk him losing the rings!

'It was important to us to have them there, as the dogs are part of our family, and I couldn't imagine them not being with us. We had one hundred human guests and two canine ones. We were really proud of William because he behaved so well. He has come so far. He wore a smart grey and white Fair Isle patterned jumper to keep him warm on the day.'

Inspector Nicky Foster believes that being adopted by Rachel and Chris was the perfect solution for William. His story has a happy ending, but she has a word of warning for people looking to bring a puppy into their home.

'Everyone who takes on a puppy should be aware of how much work and care is needed. They aren't just pretty play things. William is from a large breed, and nutrition in those early months is so vital to enable proper growth and development. He's very lucky not to have been left with serious health problems.'

To witness the end of a story such as William's – to see him content and happy – underlines what vitally important work Nicky and her colleagues do. When she first cradled the emaciated puppy in her arms, it felt as though William's days were numbered. Thanks to a whole team of people it turned out well, and William seems to know just how lucky he is.

TIPS ON HOW TO CARE FOR YOUR DOG

Alone time

OWNING A dog is incredibly fun and rewarding, but there are lots of things to consider when taking one on, such as the time and commitment needed from owners to help their pet stay happy and healthy.

Dogs are playful, sociable animals and most benefit from opportunities to spend time and play with other dogs, people and toys. Dogs shouldn't be left for long periods, but it's important that puppies learn from a young age that it's OK to be alone for short periods. The length of time a dog can be left on its own depends on the individual dog, but it's advised that they are left for no longer than four hours so that they have opportunities to exercise, go to the toilet and spend time with people. Studies have found that if you gradually introduce your dog or puppy to being left alone when they come to live with you, then you are less likely to have a problem later on.

Research also suggests that, at some point in their lives, nearly half of all pet dogs react badly to being left alone. Contrary to popular belief, dogs are not doing this because they are trying to get 'revenge' on their owners for leaving them behind — in most cases, they are genuinely distressed about being separated from their carer. If your dog barks when they are left alone, it may be because they are lonely or bored. When they are left, even if only

▶

for a short time, they need items such as chews and food toys — stuffed Kongs, for instance — to keep them busy. If possible, rather than leaving your dog alone, ask responsible friends, neighbours, dog walkers or pet sitters to help.

CHAPTER 9

Reo

E ACH AND every dog Anthony Joynes rescues is special to him, but one or two have wormed their way deep into his heart, and will always be particularly treasured. They are the dogs who have pulled through when all the odds were stacked against them, when even Anthony despaired and worried that they might not survive, let alone find forever happiness as loving, loveable family pets.

They are the dogs whose treatment and suffering was so appalling that they could be forgiven for never trusting the human race again but who, despite everything, have repaid the help they've been given many times over in love and affection. They are the gentle, devoted pets who have given their new owners rewards beyond measure for the simple act of taking them on and giving them a very different sort of home to the one where they were mistreated, and from which they needed to be rescued.

These dogs don't come along every day, but one of Anthony's special dogs is Reo, an elderly German shepherd who came within hours of being put down.

For Anthony, as it so often does, it started with a call from a concerned member of the public about a dog with a serious lower-jaw injury. As an experienced RSPCA officer, that kind of information rang alarm bells, because lower-jaw injuries are often associated with badger-fighting, and caused when badgers flip on to their backs and lock their strong teeth into the dog's lower jaw. And it takes a lot to make them let go.

However, almost to Anthony's surprise, that's not what he found when he neared the address given by the caller. As he drove his van along the row of terraced houses, he recognized the area, and when he pulled in to the kerb outside the house in question he knew he had been there before, two or three years previously, to give the owner advice and to help with her German shepherd, who had an ear infection at the time. Apart from her inflamed ear canals, the dog was generally in good condition, and the owner told Anthony that she was treating the problem. Anthony issued her with an Improvement Notice – in effect a warning – and told her the dog needed proper care from a vet.

He checked up on her ten days later and the owner, as instructed, had taken the dog to see a vet at the PDSA, who prescribed steroids and antibiotics. Anthony was satisfied that she'd done the right and responsible thing, and that the dog was getting the care she needed. He also passed on advice he'd been given himself about his own dog: when it comes to ear infections, prevention is better than cure.

He went on to explain to the owner that a deep-seated ear infection that migrates to the inner ear can cause a dog to lose its sense of balance, as well as causing deafness. He genuinely believed she had listened to him and would act on the advice.

That's why he was surprised to find himself at the same address, especially as the call from the member of the public had sounded so serious. The dog they'd described was in a bad way. When Anthony knocked on the door, a man opened it and explained that he was a friend of the owner. Made aware of their visitor, the owner then joined him at the door, and together they assured Anthony that the dog was fine and there was nothing to be concerned about. The owner almost scoffed, nonchalantly, at the idea there could be anything at all wrong with her dog.

For a moment, Anthony was almost convinced. After all, this owner had behaved responsibly last time he'd had cause to visit, and the RSPCA handle many calls with allegations that turn out to be false alarms. Sometimes they're made maliciously, sometimes with good intentions – someone thinks they've seen something that doesn't look right. Despite the time-wasting element, investigating a malicious or mistaken call is almost a breath of fresh air for Anthony, because it means that an animal is safe and well cared for, and there's nothing for him to do. One job off his long list, one less case to worry about.

However, if he was to do his job properly, he still needed to see this dog. That's when the owner told Anthony that she had booked the dog in to be euthanized that very afternoon, saying, 'It's all in hand.' She hoped this would be enough to persuade him to walk away. It wasn't. Especially after she'd changed her story so readily. Anthony persisted, asking for a second time if he could come in. The two people were reluctant to allow him into the house – not so much in the words they used, but Anthony detected in their body language that they really did not want to show him the dog. Nonetheless, eventually, they led him through to the kitchen. There was no sign of the dog, but the woman finally admitted to Anthony, 'Yes, it's quite bad. But she's going to be put down . . .'

Anthony, following the owner's gaze, went around the corner of the L-shaped room and that's when he first saw nine-year-old Reo. His hand immediately went to his forehead, which he began to rub – an involuntary habit whenever he's under stress or sees something awful. For a few seconds he couldn't find any words, he just gazed in shock and horror at the dog lying, perfectly still, on a dog bed. It was a scene that has never left him.

The dog's face and lower jaw were red raw, all the skin having been scratched away. One eye, with no fur around it, was almost closed and completely crusty, glued up and barely usable. Her ears, which should have been pricked, lay horizontal, reminding Anthony of the profile of a Vulcan bomber aircraft.

Most distressing was her demeanour. She was a broken dog. In Anthony's words, she was in 'a mind-bogglingly awful state'. Somehow she summoned the energy to get to her feet and very slowly walked across to him, her tail wagging, and rubbed her head against him. It must have been unspeakably painful, but she still had a need to seek the comfort of an affectionate touch. Perhaps it was a cry for help.

As she approached him, Anthony could see that the insides of those flattened ears were bright red, like beacons of her pain. She brought with her the pungent and unmistakeable smell of infection. Wounds from scratching covered her back and flank, and the skin where the fur had been clawed away was black and thickened.

The sight of the wretched dog was so bad that Anthony had to gulp back tears, and force his professionalism to kick in. One of the questions he is asked all the time is, 'How do you stay cool? How do you not throttle people who have been this cruel?' The answer is that he knows, as all inspectors do, that he is there to rescue the animal and to alleviate its suffering; to remove it from the neglectful or abusive house and ensure it receives swift medical attention. However, what he thinks about the owners is sometimes hard to contain.

'How did you let it get like this?' he asked, battling to suppress his anger. 'You've had help before, you know what she needs.'

The owner explained that, while she'd received free treatment from the PDSA the last time Anthony had called, she now had a job and no longer qualified for free veterinary help. It was an excuse that didn't wash with Anthony, as she clearly had enough money to feed herself, to have bought a new TV and decent furniture. It wasn't as if she was so short of money she couldn't take care of herself or her home, so surely her dog was worth the cost of a visit to a vet . . . ? He was angry as well as upset, but remained calm.

The woman also claimed, in her defence, that the condition had only flared up recently, but it didn't need a vet to see that it was serious and that the poor dog was likely to have been suffering for a long time.

'I'm taking her,' he said. It was the only conclusion, and easy to reach.

The owner repeated that she wanted Reo put to sleep, and that she was booked to be put down that afternoon. She didn't want Reo to go through the suffering that treatment would involve. This, to Anthony, sounded hypocritical, but he bit his tongue and told the woman that he wasn't in a position to say what the outcome would be in terms of Reo's treatment and chances of survival, but he was definitely taking the dog.

In his heart, Anthony suspected that euthanasia might indeed turn out to be the kindest future for poor old Reo. He had once before rescued another dog, Barney, who had had the same severity of ear canal infection, and he, sadly, had to be put to sleep. Anthony feared the same fate awaited Reo, but he was determined at least to give her a chance, and if no treatment was possible she would have a peaceful end.

He gave the owner the option of signing her over to the RSPCA, and told her that if she refused he would call the police, as the dog had to be removed as a matter of urgency. The owner acquiesced, and Reo was duly signed over to him, and as he took her out to the van, she shook her head incessantly as there was no respite from the intolerable itching deep inside her ears. Outside in the daylight, Anthony could see the full extent of Reo's self-harm, and there was more fur loss than he had previously thought. Her bottom jaw looked as if it had been eaten away.

'It's heartbreaking, because this is a manageable condition, but now the problem is so severe that if the pain can't be managed, she'll be put to sleep. It is so wrong,' he said at the time. He immediately rang vet Holly Jones to let her know that he was on his way with an emergency.

'That's not a recent flare-up,' said Holly, when Reo was led into her surgery. 'It's been going on for months. It's a vicious circle. The minute an ear gets infected it itches and they scratch, and the more they scratch, the more it itches.'

It was impossible for Holly to examine Reo fully, because every touch made the dog whimper with pain. She needed to be anaesthetized, and the howl she gave as the needle went in was an unforgettable wail of anguish, indelibly etched on the memory of everyone who heard it. It was the cry of a dog in unbearable distress, and Holly shot Anthony a look that said: 'Don't get your hopes up . . .' To all concerned, it felt that this might not be a dog they could save. Not this time.

Anthony held Reo until she was deeply under the anaesthetic and free, for the moment, from pain. When he looked down, his uniform was bloodstained from her open wounds.

Bathing Reo's raw skin, Holly delivered her verdict. 'She has a severe infection and she's covered in deep lacerations from scratching. She's been in agony. Just the lightest pressure on her was too much. Whether her ears will ever come right, I can't say. My biggest concern is whether we can get her comfortable while she heals. If we can't manage her pain, the kindest thing would be to end her suffering.'

Reo was given a large dose of painkillers, steroids and antibiotics. As the anaesthetic began to wear off, she whimpered, and Anthony could see that her life was hanging in the balance. Her immune system was so compromised that there was every chance her body wouldn't be able to withstand the treatment. Holly told him that the next forty-eight hours were absolutely critical, and Reo was kept at the vet's, under careful observation.

As Anthony drove home he couldn't stop thinking about how good-natured the poor dog had been all that day. A dog in so much pain could have been forgiven for growling or even biting anyone who tried to touch it, but Reo clearly had an amazing temperament. German shepherds often have an unfair reputation for being aggressive – perhaps because they're commonly used as guard dogs – but in Anthony's experience they're very loving. Reo's character was exceptional.

The crucial first two days passed. Reo wasn't yet out of the woods but her chances of recovery were greatly improved and her future was looking brighter. Signed off at the vet's, Anthony transported her very carefully to the RSPCA animal centre where she would be cared for during her recovery. He led her into her new room, with its large, comfy bed for her to rest on, then lay down with her and cradled her in his arms until she settled in her unfamiliar surroundings. She gave a few small whines, and he stayed with her until she drifted off to sleep and he was able to slip away.

Anthony was off duty that weekend, and he and his girl-friend, Georgia, were going up to the Lake District for a short break with her family. Anthony was so concerned about Reo that he wanted to postpone the trip, but Georgia talked sense into him, stressing how important it was for him to switch off and leave the concerns of work behind. Besides, he would still be able to keep in close contact with the animal centre: he rang each day to check on Reo's progress, and the centre staff sent pictures of her through to his phone.

On the third day of his trip, the photo Anthony received made him punch the air in joy: those ears that had reminded him of a Vulcan bomber had begun to prick up. Reo's mouth, which she had kept firmly shut at first, was now open and relaxed, with her tongue hanging out: the usual demeanour of an average, happy dog. Her whole body language had changed in such a short space of time. She looked – almost – like a normal German shepherd. She looked like a dog who was going to survive.

As soon as he was back on duty Anthony visited Reo, and she greeted him with her tail wagging exuberantly. She was still covered in scabs, and her skin must have been uncomfortable, but the horrible itching was gone, and she was no longer damaging herself. Her eye was not yet fully open, and the area around it was bald, but there was clearly no long-term damage to it, which was a huge relief. Her ears were very much improved, too, although the skin was still inflamed, and she would need to have them treated for the rest of her life.

For Anthony, the change in her was a joy to see. A broken, dejected dog had been transformed into a playful character who raced around the paddock at the animal centre with him. He was even more thrilled to hear, only a few weeks after Reo's rescue, that a family wanted to adopt her. She was all set to have the happy ending that he never dreamed could happen. He knew he had got to her in the nick of time, as the owner had indeed booked her in to be put down that very afternoon – Anthony had rung the veterinary practice in question and confirmed that this was the case. Thanks to a caring member of the public and Anthony's swift response, Reo had been given a wonderful and much-deserved reprieve.

Her next big dollop of luck came when the Corrin family turned up at the animal centre, looking for a pet. Martin and Mandy Corrin visited the centre on their own, while their three daughters, Jessica, who was thirteen at the time, and nine-year-old twins Frankie and Sam, were away on holiday with their grandparents. Martin and Mandy didn't want to get the girls' hopes up until they were sure they'd found the right dog, so they were looking around to see who was out there for them, who might fit into the heart of their family.

The whole family wanted a dog – Mandy and the girls had been asking for one for years. Martin, too, loved dogs, and both he and Mandy had grown up with pets. They often had dogs around their home, whether they were looking after Charlie (a Labrador belonging to Mandy's mum) or Billie (Martin's mum's King Charles spaniel) whenever their owners went on holiday.

For a few weeks that summer there had been a dog in the house all the time, and when the family's canine visitors finally left, the house felt empty. The couple decided that now the girls were old enough to help care for and understand a pet, the time was right. There was never any question for the Corrins about getting a rescue dog, as both Martin and Mandy felt that there are too many unwanted animals out there needing good homes. However, they had no idea what kind of dog they wanted, only that Martin was sure he didn't want a tiny little 'handbag-type' dog.

The first day after the girls left for their holiday, Martin and Mandy set off to the RSPCA Wirral & Chester Branch Animal Centre but weren't expecting to find the perfect dog immediately. However, when the staff introduced them to Reo, it was love at first sight. Gentle old Reo looked at them with her trusting eyes, and both Martin and Mandy felt the same surge of compassion and affection. There was something about her that spoke to them, and they felt immediately taken with her, that they would like to offer her the home she deserved.

They were given a brief history of her skin and ear infections, and were told that she would need ongoing treatment for her ears. What they didn't know then was just how harrowing her story had been, and until they saw photographs and video footage later on, couldn't appreciate just how serious her condition had been. That she was such a different dog now was testament to the excellent care she'd received and the miraculous recovery she'd made.

What the Corrins saw in Reo was a good-natured, energetic dog, her gentle temperament underscored when they were told that she failed police dog training when she was a puppy because she was too friendly. After all she had been through, she was naturally a bit reserved with the Corrins, but they could see she was sweet-tempered and, in the words of one of the members of staff ,'without a bad bone in her whole body'.

Martin and Mandy visited her a few times while the girls were away, and Reo began to recognize them and wagged her tail excitedly because she knew they would take her out for a walk. They sent pictures to the children, and Jessica was so overjoyed at the sight of Reo that she burst into tears.

Then came the crucial meeting with the girls: if their daughters didn't take to Reo, or she to them, it would be no good pursuing the adoption. Martin and Mandy were hoping for the same response that they had felt on seeing Reo for the first time, but nothing was certain. In the event, there was nothing to worry about. Reo was instantly great with the girls and they were thrilled to meet their new pet, although Sam was slightly in awe of her size at first. It didn't take long for Reo's gentle temperament to win her over, though, and after a couple more successful visits at the centre, the staff were happy to hand Reo over to the Corrins.

Martin and Mandy didn't mind that Reo was an older dog and that she may not have many years with them. Mandy felt strongly that she wanted to take on a dog that other people might reject, and because of her age, the re-homing staff at the animal centre had feared that Reo would struggle to find a forever home. The general feeling among prospective owners is that younger dogs make the best pets because they have less baggage, may be easier to train, and will be with the owners for many more years.

Mandy's feeling was that after Reo had come so close to death, it would have been very sad indeed if she had to spend the rest of her days in kennels instead of with a loving family. Everyone who worked at the centre was delighted that Reo had struck so lucky.

So was Anthony, who also always worries when he rescues an older dog that their future may not pan out as well as it would for a younger one. He salutes all the families like the Corrins, who are happy to take on dogs and give them love and comfort in the later stage of their lives. Sometimes the stars simply align.

'It was a no-brainer for us,' said Martin. 'We wanted a dog and she wanted a home, and when we saw her we knew she was the one for us. Her age was never a factor.'

The day the Corrins took Reo home to live with them, she was a little distressed, probably because over the past few weeks she'd experienced so many changes and had to get to know so many new people. Another new environment was initially a step too far. She ripped her dog bed to pieces, then set about demolishing the dog toys the girls had bought for her. The Corrins remained calm and loving, however, and her anxiety soon evaporated. Her physical problems, however, continued.

'Her ears aren't perfect and they never will be, but she's a million times better than in those awful pictures of her when she was first rescued,' says Mandy. Because they adopted Reo with a chronic condition, the costs for her treatments are met by the RSPCA.

In the early days, Reo had to visit the vet every two or three weeks to have her ears treated, but that's gone down to only every couple of months, as much of the care can now be done at home: Mandy is able to administer the drops herself and flush Reo's ears out every day. At first Reo hated having her ears touched, and it took Mandy a while to win her trust. She would yelp even if someone brushed against them. She still cries when they are being cleaned, but she sits still, as if she knows what is happening is for her own good, and that she'll get a treat afterwards.

If there is a build-up of pus for any reason and Reo starts to scratch again, she goes straight back to the vet. This is the kind of swift action that her first owner should have taken, and her inaction back then means that Reo is now on a permanent regime of steroids. Martin and Mandy know that her ear condition will be with her for the rest of her life, and they try not to think about the previous owner who allowed it to become so bad.

Like many people who rescue dogs, although they hate the thought of anyone neglecting such a beautiful, good-natured animal, they also know that they would never have met their wonderful pet if she hadn't needed to be rescued. It's a curious conundrum.

Martin took a week off work when Reo first came home, to help her get used to her new surroundings. On her first night she cried and whimpered, which isn't uncommon behaviour in a re-homed dog, and he spent hours going up and down the stairs to comfort her. Now she sleeps on blankets on the upstairs landing – it's as if she likes to keep her eyes on the bedrooms, and stay close to all the people she now loves devotedly. Jessica and Frankie happily encourage her on to their beds, and she sometimes sneaks in with Martin and Mandy, too.

Martin works from home much of the time, so he's able to take her for walks, her greatest pleasure in life. As soon as he enters a room, Reo's head goes up, hoping he'll get her lead. Because of her size and the general misconception about the nature of German shepherds, Martin finds that when he walks her, some other dog owners treat her warily until they realize she's a placid softie, so he keeps her on a lead until he knows that others in the vicinity are happy with her presence. He understands that such a big dog, with a loud, deep bark, can be off-putting.

On a recent Scottish holiday with the family, Reo was happy to walk for up to two hours a day and, although she needed to lie down afterwards, it didn't wipe her out. Martin knows that if he'd rattled her lead at any point, she'd have been up and ready for even more. She's also happy just to play in the garden and in the house, and when she's feeling particularly full of beans she races up and down the hallway. It's a remarkable feat for a dog who, not so long ago, struggled to walk, and for the family it's an insight into the dog she must have been when she was much younger.

'I sometimes wonder what she was like as a young dog,' said Martin. 'We've only known her as an old girl, but she must have been a real bundle of energy when she was younger.'

Despite her age and a creeping problem with arthritis in her hips, which is not unusual in elderly German shepherds, Reo's still a very strong animal, as Martin discovered to his cost when he was out walking her with his mother, brother and the twins. Reo was on an extendable lead at the time, and as Martin was bending down to pick up her deposit in a poo bag, Frankie called her. Reo took off towards her, pulling Martin over, and leaving him with a bad shoulder for a few days. He laughs at the mishap now, glad that Reo is so happy within the family group that she wanted to get to Frankie at any cost.

Every evening, somewhere between 9 and 10 p.m., Reo always springs to life and thrusts her nose into Martin's lap, reminding him that it's time for her last walk of the day.

When she's not out walking, Reo's other great love is cuddling up on the couch with whichever member of the family happens to be there. She loves being petted and stroked, and the girls love burying their faces into her thick coat, which has now completely recovered. It's a scene of perfect contentment but it took a while for Reo to learn the rules of family life.

She used to snatch treats when they were offered, but she has learnt patience, although she still takes any food that is left within her reach, and if you walk past her with a sandwich in your hand, beware. On one occasion she gobbled down most of a loaf of bread, and at her first Christmas with the family she demolished four chocolate selection boxes, complete with wrappers. Fortunately, she was taken to the vet quickly, and luckily, apart from a bloated stomach and feeling a bit sorry for herself for a couple of days, no serious harm was done. It taught everyone to make sure to keep anything edible out of her reach.

During an outbreak of fungi along the grass verges near to their home, Martin had to use all his strength to hold her back from devouring them. Her ravenous appetite makes Mandy and Martin wonder if she was short of food in her previous home, and feels the need to grab it when she can. It's the kind of behaviour the owners of re-homed dogs see quite frequently.

One of the proudest moments for the whole family was when Reo came first in the Best Rescue class at the RSPCA Wirral & Chester Branch's summer fair. The girls promptly bought her a Wonder Woman bandana to celebrate her win, although Reo was probably more thrilled with the large pack of Bonios that was offered as first prize.

When Martin occasionally has to leave her at the vet for treatment, he describes the family home as feeling as if 'there is a gaping hole in the house'. He speaks for all the family when he says it feels as if she has always been with them. They can't remember life without her. It's weird to think of a time when she wasn't part of their unit.

For Anthony, it's the best happy-ever-after he could have dreamt of for the dog he feared would have to be put to sleep. Whenever he bumps into Reo at the vet's, or at events like the RSPCA summer fair, she always greets him ecstatically, as though she has a deep memory of the man who stepped in to make her life immeasurably better.

Anthony won't forget her previous owner in a hurry. She was taken to court where she pleaded guilty, and showed a lot of remorse in court for causing the suffering. She received an eighteen-week suspended prison sentence and a lifetime ban from keeping animals. 'Part of her punishment is that she will live with this for the rest of her life,' declares Anthony. 'I'll never, ever forget my first sight of Reo. The moment I don't get emotionally involved in a job like this one is the moment I should look for another career.'

When Reo's story was broadcast on *The Dog Rescuers*, Anthony received letters, tweets and emails thanking him for his work. All the inspectors who appear on the programme get a hugely favourable response from the public, who see clearly the extraordinary work that they do all the time, tirelessly and with great passion. One viewer even thanked him in person for all the dogs the many RSPCA officers save. She also revealed that she used to live near Reo, back when she was a younger dog, and that Reo used to be in good health. So it seems that things only got out of control for her owner later on. It doesn't make the case any better, but it shows the owner's remorse was probably genuine, not just an act for the court. It's a powerful reminder, however, that looking after a dog is a full-time job, for life.

TIPS ON HOW TO CARE FOR YOUR DOG

Ear conditions

EAR PROBLEMS are really common in dogs; in fact, a 2014 recent study found that ear canal conditions were the most common health issue seen in dogs. Because of this, it's recommended that all dogs have an annual veterinary health check to help detect any potential problems as early and as effectively as possible, and also that owners check their dog's ears regularly for any sign of problems.

There can be many causes of health issues in dogs' ears, including mites, allergies and foreign bodies. Signs that a dog might have a problem are scratching or rubbing their ears, or shaking their head. If an owner thinks their dog may be affected, it's really important to ask a vet for advice as soon as possible, as ear conditions can be painful and cause long-term problems without prompt treatment.

Regular checks can be introduced as part of the dog's grooming routine. It provides a good opportunity to carry out a general health check, looking for evidence of parasites, such as fleas or ticks, and removing any grass seeds which could have become trapped in the dog's paws or in their ears.

Grooming is beneficial because it removes dirt, dead skin and loose fur, and gives owners a chance to check their dog's general body condition, to see if their pet is the right weight (see page 51), and to spot any new or unusual

▶

lumps or bumps which might need further attention. If grooming is introduced positively and slowly, it can be a great way of keeping an eye on your pet's health, but also of giving them some extra attention, developing and strengthening the bond between you.

CHAPTER 10

Molly

L IFE CAN sometimes be very unfair. Poor Molly, a little terrier, had already escaped one unhappy home and seemed well on the road to making a full recovery. She was waiting to start the next chapter of her life in a new home, when she was hit with something far worse: the discovery of a serious health condition that could end her life at any time, and gave her a life expectancy of only a few months. What had she done to deserve such terrible luck?

Molly is a sweet, loving, happy soul, and everyone who knows her couldn't believe life had dealt her two terrible blows. However, thanks to the amazing work of a specialist vet, very generous members of the public donating money to pay for her care, and a whole load of TLC, today, Molly is racing around full of beans. She loves playing with her new owners, and when she's feeling a bit lazy, her favourite occupation is lying stretched out in the garden. Especially if the sun is shining. Pretty little Molly is a real sun worshipper.

Molly was first found by RSPCA Inspector Herchy Boal, after a tip-off from a member of the public about a house where five dogs were living. According to the anonymous caller, one of the dogs was grossly overweight and another had hardly any fur. Herchy visited the address, and although the owner of the dogs was unfriendly and made it clear Herchy's presence was unwelcome, the woman eventually agreed to let Herchy come in and see the animals.

Three of the dogs were fine, and gave Herchy no cause for concern. A fourth, however, was a very old, arthritic collie, who was in a state of collapse when Herchy saw him. She warned the owner that if he was not back up on his feet within twenty-four hours, he would need to be looked at by a vet. Herchy could see the elderly dog was settled and very attached to his owner, who clearly loved him too, so Herchy felt he was in the right place to be cared for, and simply told the owner she would be coming back to check on him again the following day.

That left one other dog, poor little Molly. Herchy knew at a glance that she needed treatment immediately. The small, white terrier was tearing at herself constantly, clawing at her inflamed and bright red skin, and the fur on her ears, face, belly and down her legs had been scraped away through incessant scratching. There were bloody spots where she had ripped through her skin in a desperate bid to get rid of the itching, and scabs where her body had struggled to heal itself. She clearly had a serious skin condition and was in a very distressed state. The situation was way beyond simply giving the owner advice on what to do in order to care for her dog. Molly needed to see a vet straight away, and it was Herchy's duty to make sure that this happened.

Despite the owner's protestations that the skin condition had only worsened badly over the past few days and that she had already taken the little dog to a vet about it, Herchy could see it was a long-standing problem — and when she checked out the owner's story later, she discovered that the woman hadn't been telling the truth. Molly hadn't seen a vet in the past six months.

The owner was devastated when Herchy informed her that she was going to take five-year-old Molly to a vet. At first she refused point blank to let Herchy remove her from the house, and the RSPCA inspector had to warn her that, if necessary, she would call the police in order to seize the dog, so that it could be taken to a vet straight away. A call to the police is always a last resort, though, and Herchy spent a patient forty-five minutes cajoling the owner, who was terribly upset and crying, to allow her to take Molly away for medical care. It was fortunate that a friend of the owner's was also in the house at the time, and helped Herchy to persuade the woman that it was the right thing to do, for Molly's sake.

The owner wouldn't sign Molly over into the RSPCA's ownership at this stage, which is what Herchy ideally wanted to happen, but eventually the woman tearfully agreed to let the poor little terrier go with Herchy to a vet.

For Herchy, it was a difficult case. The owner had other personal problems in her life. She clearly loved her animals, the environment in which they were living was clean, and it was obvious that they were being well fed, but the bottom line was that the woman had neglected to get treatment for Molly, who was suffering very badly. The terrier's acute distress was obvious, and the owner had ignored it. This amounted to a crime, and it was Herchy's duty to act. As she took the little dog away, it was hard to tell who was more distraught — the owner, or Molly, who was in such pain she couldn't focus on anything except the persistent itching. The situation required careful handling and Herchy's experience guided her through.

When vet Jack McHale saw how agitated Molly was, he agreed without hesitation that Herchy had been right to bring her in. He could feel when he touched Molly that her skin was on fire, and it was impossible to examine her ears because they were so badly infected the ear canals were blocked. Jack knew that trying to insert a scope into her ears to assess the damage would be cruel, as the pain would be so intense it would no doubt make the little dog scream. Looking at her ears would have to wait. In any case, that was just one of her problems.

Jack gave the little dog antibiotics to fight her infections and painkillers to ease the torture of her itching, and he took skin scrapes to determine whether there were mites or fleas causing her irritation. Little Molly was checked into the vet's for an overnight stay, and settled down on a clean and comfortable bed with obvious relief as the medication kicked in and soothed her urge to scratch. No longer kept awake by the irresistible need to claw at her damaged skin, it was probably her first full night's sleep for weeks.

Herchy, too, was able to sleep soundly, knowing that her small charge was in good hands. She made the owner aware of what was happening and, as promised, called back the next day, to check on the elderly collie. Thankfully, he was now up and about, and Herchy, satisfied that he was well, was happy to leave him there.

A few weeks later, she conducted a formal interview with the owner about Molly's condition, and at this point the owner agreed to sign Molly over to the RSPCA. She received a formal caution relating to Molly's neglect.

Herchy has been an RSPCA inspector for eighteen years, coming into the profession with a degree in agriculture and a background as a veterinary nurse. It was a television programme about the work of the charity and its inspectors that sparked her interest in working for the RSPCA, and she hasn't ever regretted joining their ranks, finding a huge amount of job satisfaction and fulfilment on a daily basis.

'Every day is different. Sometimes I'm dealing with outright cruelty, or deliberate neglect. Sometimes I simply need to give owners some advice on how to care for their pets. Molly falls into a difficult area, because the owner clearly cared but was simply not able or willing, because of her own problems, to get Molly the help she needed. My priority is always the animal – that's my job – but sometimes I feel for the owners,' she said.

Vet Jack, in the meantime, confirmed that Molly is a dog prone to various allergies. It's more common in white dogs than in dogs with other coat colours, and needs lifelong management – Molly will always need medication. If the owner had taken Molly for a quick trip to a vet when she first started scratching, the problem would have been diagnosed sooner and it would have been possible to have kept it under control. Not responding quickly enough allowed the allergic reaction to take hold.

Now that she had been given the right treatment, things perked up straight away for Molly – the fierce itching stopped, her scabs healed, her fur began to grow back and, to cap it off, she became a firm favourite with all the staff and volunteers when she settled in at the Coventry RSPCA Animal Centre. Herchy was thrilled to visit her and see what an amazing transformation the right care had made to Molly's miserable life. Her little mate greeted her with her head cocked inquisitively to one side.

'When I met her before, all she could think about was scratching – she was in so much agony. Now she's thinking about food and play – all the normal doggy things.'

Just as the sun was shining on Molly for the first time in a long while, she was dealt another, much more serious blow. The RSPCA routinely neuter all dogs that come into their care and, when Molly was taken to the vet's for her operation, the regular check-up carried out beforehand showed something alarming. Little Molly's heart rate was very slow: only 45 beats per minute, compared to the 80 to 140 that is normal for a dog her age. Crucially, when she exercised, her heart was unable to increase its rate accordingly.

Molly urgently needed to see an expert veterinary cardiologist, to assess if anything could be done to help her. However, specialist services don't come cheap, so the animal centre launched an appeal to help with the funding.

By complete coincidence, Chris Linney and his wife, Katherine, with their young son, James, in tow, called in at the centre around that time to look at the possibility of re-homing a cat to live with them and their Hungarian Vizsla, Izzy. Walking along the row of kennels, Chris spotted the sign 'Molly's Heart Appeal', along with a notice that the little white terrier wasn't available for re-homing because of her heart condition.

It was a lucky encounter because Chris happens to be a veterinary cardiologist and Katherine is also a vet. Curious about Molly, he asked the staff about her condition, and they explained how she needed an assessment to see what treatment, if any, could help her. He replied that he would see what help he could give personally, and fortunately there was enough money already raised for Molly to be assessed at the clinic where Chris is the head cardiology surgeon – the Willows Veterinary Centre and Referral Service in Solihull, West Midlands. The centre, as well as dealing with local patients, receives cases from all over the UK, and has a range of specialist services, including a cutting-edge cardiology department.

When Chris checked Molly's ECG, which shows the electrical activity of the heart, he soon confirmed what her local vet had diagnosed: her heartbeat was very slow and, without help, the risk of sudden death would be permanently close by. When a heart beats abnormally slowly and does not increase with exertion, it gradually becomes enlarged and dilated, and eventually it goes into failure. Put under any pressure – if Molly exercised, for example – her little heart could give out at any moment. Even if she only rested and sat quietly, with her heart in its current state she only had a short life expectancy. Without surgery, Chris assessed, she might not make it to the end of the year. Molly's rare condition is known technically as bradycardia, and it needed to be dealt with as soon as possible. A pacemaker was her only chance.

Molly's pacemaker would be an electrical device that stimulates her heart to beat at a normal rate, and would be similar to those that have been fitted in human heart patients since the 1960s. Fitting a pacemaker is not something an ordinary vet can undertake – Molly needed to return to the Willows for highly specialized care.

Chris knew Molly needed the operation urgently, but it was going to be expensive. While the RSPCA pays for most of the veterinary care of the animals it takes on, to spend

£3,500 on one dog would seriously deplete the funds available for many other cases. So the low-key appeal was stepped up. Local publicity ran with the message: 'Please help heal Molly's broken heart.'

The little dog had already featured in an episode of *The Dog Rescuers* with Herchy, which had followed her removal from her home and the medical care she received for her skin condition, but her new plight really struck a chord with people. Donations poured in, including from her previous owner, who had been so devastated to lose her. Meanwhile, Molly was blithely enjoying her comfortable life at the animal centre, loving her walks and, with no more skin problems, she was blissfully unaware of the huge wave of concern about her health. The target amount was reached very quickly as the money flooded in, and she was promptly whisked back to the Willows for the tricky operation.

Chris would have carried out the op anyway, even if the funds had only dribbled in. The Willows is a big practice and can, occasionally, arrange long-term instalment payments for acute conditions. However, thanks to the generosity of the public, there was enough money to pay.

It was Valentine's Day 2017 when Molly was taken into the state-of-the-art operating theatre. Pinned to her kennel at the hospital centre was a Valentine's card, decorated with a big red heart, sent with love from all her friends and admirers back at the RSPCA Coventry Animal Centre. The centre's staff and volunteers went about their business that day with their fingers crossed that one of their favourite residents would make it through major heart surgery, and soon be back to enjoy her favourite hobby of sunbathing.

Chris, who qualified as a vet in 2008, has been a cardiologist since 2010, and in that time has fitted more than one hundred pacemakers. He was attracted to veterinary cardiology because he'd always been fascinated by the complexities of the heart, and by the way modern veterinary science can allow major problems to be tackled in minimally invasive ways – and this includes fitting pacemakers.

Dogs can suffer from many of the same heart problems as human beings, and in almost all cases similar treatment options are available for them, although heart transplants are never carried out on dogs, partly because dogs come in so many different breeds, shapes and sizes. Cats, which are generally much smaller animals, are more difficult to treat and Chris has only once installed a feline pacemaker. Heart conditions like Molly's are diagnosed very infrequently in cats, partly because they are happy to rest and do very little if they feel unwell, whereas dogs will carry on exercising and putting strain on their hearts.

Slow or irregular heartbeats are rare conditions, even among dogs with heart problems. Only one in two hundred of Chris's patients need a pacemaker, making the devices very rare indeed among the dog population in general. The Willows is one of only a handful of practices carrying out the surgery, and at any one time they have between twenty and thirty surviving patients with a pacemaker fitted. The surgery has been available for dogs almost as long as it has been for humans, and techniques have improved enormously over the years. Most importantly, the size of the battery has shrunk and its lifespan has extended.

Scrubbed in and wearing a jaunty surgical cap decorated with pictures of dogs, Chris began work on an anaesthetized Molly. His aim was to pass a lead down her jugular vein through to her heart. The lead has tiny fishhooks attached to its tip, which anchor it at the bottom of the heart. The lead is then connected to a small battery, implanted under the skin.

With a lifespan of ten years, the battery could easily outlive Molly, but it's very straightforward to replace should anything go wrong before then. It's possible that an active little terrier like Molly may wear it out more quickly.

The electrical impulses sent from the battery through the lead are programmed for a normal heart rate, and would make sure that Molly's heart behaved normally, giving her the chance to live energetically and fully for the standard expected lifespan of a terrier like her.

Chris started by making a small incision above Molly's jugular vein on the left-hand side of her neck, through which the lead could be passed straight down to her heart. It's a very delicate operation, and if the jugular vein is traumatized in any way there could be profuse bleeding, so Chris proceeded cautiously. At first things were going well, but then Chris hit a major snag. The lead would not travel where he wanted it to go.

'There's something slightly different about Molly's anatomy on her left side,' Chris explained. When the lead was passed along the vein on that side of her neck it was hitting a blind end, and not getting as far as the heart. It was a problem Chris had encountered only once before. The jugular veins on either side of Molly's neck both feed into her heart, but this one, on the left-hand side, was taking an unexpected detour, and the soft lead can't cope with bends. It needs to follow a fairly straight path. Chris carefully stitched up the incision he had made and moved on to his back-up plan, going in from the other side of her neck. If this second attempt hadn't worked, the only option left would have been to open Molly's chest and attach the lead straight to the heart, a more dangerous and difficult procedure, from which Molly would take much longer to recover, and one which vets rarely have to perform.

As the unconscious dog was carefully turned over, Chris started work again, with another small incision, and he and the theatre staff were anxious to see if Molly's plumbing on this side was normal and would allow access to the heart. Thankfully, after a breath-holding moment when the lead was first passed into the vein, everything went off perfectly, and the lead was safely anchored.

One of the theatre nurses helped to test whether the lead was working by using a piece of equipment called a pacemaker analyser, which can interrogate the lead to check if it has embedded in the right place. Once it had been checked, the lead was then attached to the small battery, about the size of a watch face, which had been implanted under the skin in Molly's neck. Molly's heartbeat immediately climbed to a regular 60 to 80 beats per minute, even as she lay immobile from the anaesthetic. The operation had taken an hour and a half, nearly double the time usually necessary for a straightforward pacemaker insertion. At times it had been challenging, but Chris was pleased with the result.

'Typically, a dog of her size should have a heartbeat of 120 to 140 beats per minute when exercising, and the pacemaker allows Molly to go up to 160, so she should be able to lead a full, energetic, long and happy life,' he said.

A sleepy little pup was returned to her kennel to doze off the anaesthetic, and the staff and volunteers at Coventry Animal Centre were thrilled when the phone rang to let them know that she had survived the surgery, and that the operation had been a success. It was the Valentine's Day present they had all been waiting for.

Whenever Chris checked on Molly over the next three days, her heartbeat was normal, and the pacemaker analyser showed the lead was bedding into the heart correctly. The first three days are the most crucial, because that's when most complications occur. She was almost out of the woods. However, when Molly was discharged back to the animal centre, it was with strict instructions to take it very easy for the first month, so that the lead could become securely embedded.

Back at the animal centre, Molly seemed completely unfazed by her surgery, but because she needed to be carefully rested and kept comfortable, it was decided she needed a foster carer rather than to go back into kennels. The RSPCA didn't have to look far to find one: Amanda Hull, the head receptionist at the animal centre, stepped forward. Amanda lives in a flat on the centre premises with her partner, Pete Padington. Amanda and Pete both love dogs, and so when Amanda heard that Molly needed fostering, she was quick to volunteer.

Amanda had been working at the centre for more than four years, and before that she had volunteered there for two years. Her job involves meeting dogs when they first come to the centre and seeing them when they leave for their new homes, but since moving in to the flat on the site, she has had more interaction with the dogs who live there while they wait to be re-homed, and it's an aspect of the job she loves. She helps shut the dogs in at night, and she and Pete, who gives her a hand, got to know and love Molly because the stubborn little terrier was so attached to her bed in her outside run that she refused to move into her inside bed at night.

'She'd sit there looking at us, as much as to say, "What do you mean, time for bed? I *am* in bed." She just loved being outside,' remembers Amanda.

On a few occasions, Pete had to crawl through the trapdoor from the inside kennel to the run to pick her up and bring her in. He and Amanda had both laughed at the obstinate, loveable little dog, and she'd become a firm favourite with them, especially as she was a long-term resident. Like the rest of the staff, they were on tenterhooks when she went away for her heart surgery.

By the time Molly came out of hospital, Amanda and Pete had finished most of the refurbishment they were doing on their accommodation, so it was a good time for them to take on the dog's care. Amanda had always wanted to be a foster carer, and Molly was the obvious first candidate. Unlike Pete, Amanda hadn't been brought up with dogs for pets, although she'd always loved animals, and as soon as she left home she made up for the lack of them in her life by taking on rabbits, hamsters and mice. Working full time, it was difficult to have a dog, the pet she really longed for. As time went on, the feeling of wanting one in her life was reinforced through getting to know Pete's family dog, a lovely Staffie called Chaos. For a time, the couple lived with Pete's parents, and life in a household with a dog was a wonderful experience for Amanda.

'There's nothing as special as coming home to a dog who is always happy to see you. You talk to them and they always listen, and they don't argue or contradict you.'

When Chaos died at the age of fourteen, after a long and happy life, both Pete and Amanda decided that one day they would have another furry friend to share their lives. The job at the animal centre had given Amanda a lot more knowledge of animals, and dogs in particular, and she also completed a two-year animal welfare course while working there.

Molly took to life at home with Amanda and Pete immediately, but they were dismayed to discover that the little dog's troubles weren't over yet. She is such a sensitive thing that she reacted badly to the stitches, and had to go back to hospital for another full anaesthetic to replace one with a suture made from a different material. Then she had a third anaesthetic to remove another stitch. The adverse reaction had meant that her body wanted to expel the stitches and, when this didn't happen, a hole known as a discharging tract formed next to the stitches, and could have become infected if the stitch hadn't been removed.

Amanda and Pete found it difficult to keep the patient calm and quiet while she recovered from her operations. Molly didn't like being in her crate and was grumpy because she was so desperate to be out and about doing things. She was also under orders not to climb the stairs, but at the slightest chance she'd be dashing up.

What impressed Molly's new carers the most was her resilience. She'd endured so much and, even now, everyday life entails a lot of care to treat her allergies. Amanda has to clean her ears every night, and she has special wipes provided by the vet to keep her feet clean, in case something she picks up on them triggers her allergies again. Fortunately, Molly is very obliging and happy to have her feet and ears cleaned – she appears to enjoy the fuss.

When she first came home with the couple, Molly was on seven tablets a day, a cocktail of antibiotics to prevent infection after the operation, as well as steroids and medication to stop her itching. Gradually, Amanda and Pete have weaned her down to two steroid tablets a day but, from time to time, if they see any sign of her allergies flaring up, they increase the dosage. They take her to the vet regularly to make sure it's all going well, and they know that she'll always be on medication – but she takes her tablets happily. There's no doubt she's smart enough to understand that they're doing her good.

Chris's wife, Katherine, is the vet who now manages Molly's skin condition, so he's able to get regular updates on her condition. When he and his family visited the animal centre about eleven months after her op, Chris was astonished by how well she looked. When he'd operated, her fur had still been patchy and her skin looked sore, but she's now completely changed. For him, giving a dog like Molly such a big helping hand, saving her life and allowing her to enjoy her time with her new family, is the greatest joy of his job.

To begin with, Molly went back for a check-up on her pacemaker with the analyser every three months, but that dropped to every six months and will soon be just once a year. In the meantime, Amanda and Pete have to make sure that if she goes to a normal vet for routine treatment, the vet is aware that she cannot have injections in or have blood taken from her neck.

After just a few weeks, the moment came when Molly was well enough to go back into the kennels for re-homing. However, Amanda and Pete could not part with her. They were so used to her snuggling up with them on the sofa and sharing their bed, burrowing down under the duvet when she got the chance, they could not face the prospect of her going to another home. Worse, before a re-homing could take place, little Molly would have seen Amanda regularly when she was shutting the dogs in at night, and Amanda would have felt she'd be betraying all their mutual love and devotion. It was unthinkable. So she and Pete applied to be her new, permanent owners, and they're both very happy to know she will now be with them for ever.

Molly, despite being a very loveable dog around human beings, can be a bit tetchy with other dogs, so Amanda can't keep her in the reception area of the animal centre when she's at work. Molly likes to tell other dogs that they're not welcome, so it would be unfair on the poor, traumatized rescue dogs being brought in to the centre to have to cope with her telling them off.

However, living on-site means that Amanda is able to pop back to the flat during the day to see her, and Pete's work as a freelance vehicle mechanic means that he's sometimes around at home with her too. On her own, Molly's happy to just curl up and sleep, but when Amanda and Pete are at home she loves it – particularly when they work in the garden. She'll follow them around and find favourite sunny spots to lie in. Because she's white and has hyper-sensitive skin, Amanda and Pete have to limit the amount of sunbathing she does, otherwise she'd be basking from sunrise to sunset and doing herself damage.

In the evening, when the couple go around the kennels shutting in the thirty dogs that live there, Molly accompanies them, sniffing about and wandering through the grounds. Amanda is working on socializing her with other dogs, as they'd love to foster more, but it's a slow process. At the moment they can't, because Molly wouldn't welcome another dog into the household. Her early life might have been spent living with four other dogs, but now that she has the undivided attention of Amanda and Pete, she's definitely not keen on sharing.

It's understandable but it's a shame, though Amanda is confident it will get better. She feels passionately about the need for rescue dogs to be fostered, so she's working hard on improving Molly's proprietorial behaviour.

On occasion, dogs have been tied to the front gates of the animal centre and abandoned, often left for hours before anyone sees them, because the centre has a long driveway. Sometimes boxes of kittens are left outside too. The centre is licensed for thirty dogs and thirty cats, but that number can be doubled if suitable foster carers can be found. If animals are the subject of a court case, where the owner has refused to sign them over to the RSPCA, it can be twelve months before they are eligible for re-homing and it's not good for them to be in kennels all that time, particularly if they are young and at a critical stage of their development.

Amanda loves her job. 'I am proud every day to put my uniform on. It is not a job you can switch off from. Sometimes in the evening I find myself giving medication to poorly kittens. I'm lucky that Pete understands and is more than happy to help out.'

Pete adds, 'In my regular job I can always say that I'll come back tomorrow. If the weather makes roads unpassable, I can put my work off. But looking after animals has to be done, and I understand that. I enjoy it, too.'

Molly also enjoys her new life with Amanda and Pete.

'I cannot sing her praises enough,' says Amanda. 'She's my little ray of sunshine. After everything she's been through, she deserves this life.'

TIPS ON HOW TO CARE FOR YOUR DOG

Safety at home

THERE IS no one 'perfect' way to care for all dogs because every dog and every situation is different. Some dogs require special diets and others require certain medications to keep them healthy. However, all dogs have the same basic needs:

- a suitable environment;
- a suitable diet;
- to be able to exhibit normal behaviour patterns;
- to be housed with, or apart from, other animals;
- to be protected from pain, suffering, injury and disease.

Providing a suitable environment includes offering somewhere warm and safe to live – all dogs need a comfortable, dry and draught-free place where they can rest undisturbed. This could be a crate in a quiet area of the house that they always have access to (i.e. the door is left open).

Dogs are inquisitive, but there are some items in the home and garden that can pose a risk to them. For example, some of the most common poisons that affect dogs are chocolate, ibuprofen, and slug and snail pellets. Preventing your dog from coming into contact with poisonous substances and treating any accidental poisonings quickly and appropriately is an important part of responsible pet ownership.

▶

In the home

- Keep houseplants in containers placed where your dog cannot reach them. Collect and dispose of any fallen leaves or petals.
- Keep pesticides, such as rat bait, away from any areas to which your dog has access.
- Watch dogs closely when they are running free indoors.

Outside

- Ensure housing and exercise areas are free from, and not overhung by, poisonous plants.
- Ensure your dog's water supply cannot become contaminated, and change it regularly.

What to do if you think your dog has been poisoned

- Stay calm. Remove your dog from the source of poison.
- Contact your vet for advice immediately; inform them when, where and how the poisoning occurred.
- Follow your vet's advice. If you are advised to take your dog to the vet, do so quickly and calmly.

Never 'watch and wait' in any case of suspected poisoning. If you think your pet has been affected, act fast and contact a vet for advice immediately. See rspca.org.uk/whatwedo/care/vetcare for more information.

CHAPTER 11

Buddy (aka Socks)

THESE DAYS, Anthony Joynes bumps into Buddy from time to time at the vet's, and he's very happy to see the dog he rescued safe in the care of a family who clearly dotes on him. It is, he says, the kind of result he'd like for every dog he deals with. If there was ever a dog that deserved a fresh start in a home where he is looked after and loved, though, it's Buddy. When Anthony first met him, it was a very different story.

With tears in his eyes, Anthony was crouched down on the floor of a dirty and cramped living room, one hand resting protectively on the back of an elderly dog who had an enormous lump on his side and an ulcerated tumour under his tail. Bald and blind, the yeasty smell of infection coming from the animal pervaded the house – it was so potent, Anthony had been able to detect it from outside the front door.

On the couch, cowering and whimpering, with his tail between his legs, was another dog, the fur on his face, neck and much of his body missing, and his claws so long that they curled around in spirals. As Anthony approached the animal, it lifted its front paw – body language displayed by dogs who are worried and anxious. It was a gesture from a dog so badly neglected he could be forgiven for snarling at anyone who came near.

Anthony was with the owner of the dogs, who had reluctantly allowed him and another inspector in to his home to see the animals. The RSPCA had been alerted to the fact that there were neglected dogs in the flat by six different phone calls from concerned members of the public, but on an earlier visit to the property, Anthony's colleague had been unable to gain access.

The RSPCA inspectors have no power of entry, and can only call the police to help them if they know for certain there is a suffering animal inside. Luckily, a quick-witted member of the public had managed to take a photograph of the younger, bald dog when it had appeared outside on the balcony of the flat, and it was clear, even from the fuzzy snap, that he was in desperate need of help.

So this time, when Anthony's knocks at the front door were ignored, he called through the letterbox. 'I need to speak to you urgently about your dogs. I've seen the state of one of them. I'll give you a minute to get yourself together, mate, and open the door. Otherwise I'll have to call the police. We need to see these dogs properly.'

At first, the owner opened the door just part of the way, bringing the younger of the two dogs with him.

'Can you take him?' he asked. 'I can't afford to look after him.'

It was a clear admission that something was terribly wrong, but it wasn't enough to satisfy Anthony. He had to insist on going inside, into a dingy room with old blankets strewn on the floor. Pulling back a curtain and allowing daylight in, he saw the two dogs clearly, both of them obviously in urgent need of medical attention. The owner said he'd been treating the skin condition of Socks, the younger dog, but it didn't take a vet's eye to see that wasn't the case, and that the poor dog was itching and scratching and ripping away his own fur.

Despite Socks' poor condition, it was the old guy, Patch, who broke Anthony's heart. The lump on his side was bigger than a tennis ball and he, too, had a lot of his fur missing. When Anthony lifted his tail he caught sight of the open, festering tumour.

'How can you go to sleep at night, knowing he has that?' Anthony asked the owner, incredulous, and with tears filling his eyes.

The man explained the dog was fifteen years old and that he'd owned him all his life. The way he spoke about him suggested that he cared about him very much.

'I know you don't want to give him up,' Anthony sympathized. He could see the owner was very attached to the dog, despite being guilty of terrible cruelty by neglecting him so badly. 'But he's in a horrific state. How can you live with it? I'm taking both dogs today.' There was no way he was leaving without them. Had the owner objected, Anthony simply would have called the police to help seize the dogs.

One of the difficulties Anthony and his fellow RSPCA

inspectors face is when they come across cases such as Patch and Socks. Sometimes they meet owners who are battling physical or mental health problems, or dealing with personal issues such as unemployment. They haven't deliberately inflicted cruelty on the animals in their care, but have neglected their animals for so long that they've ended up in a terrible state.

'I try to be fair. But in this case it was hard to hide my frustration, because from the guy's balcony I could see the rooftop of a veterinary surgery, not more than a couple of hundred yards away. When money is a problem, the PDSA will treat animals for free, or at a discounted rate, for anyone who meets the eligibility criteria. If you can't take your dog for free treatment, you've made a decision that you're not going to help it, and that's unforgivable.'

The owner agreed to sign Patch and Socks — both of indeterminate breed but believed to be collie crosses — into the ownership of the RSPCA, and Anthony and his colleague carefully took the animals out to their vans. Patch was confused, and had to be guided out because he couldn't see, his misery apparent in every shivering inch of his feeble body.

Socks, too, was disorientated, and clearly not used to being taken outside. Anthony could see from the length of his claws and the state of his skin that he'd endured months and months of neglect. His skin was crawling with fleas, and had thickened and darkened where the skin had come away, a condition known as lichenification but colloquially called 'elephant skin' because it looks like the hide of an elephant. Once the skin has thickened, it can harbour bacteria and yeast infections, which in turn make the itching and scratching worse. It's a vicious circle.

When Anthony got the bewildered dogs to vet Holly Jones, he took Patch into her surgery first, as his suffering was the most urgent. It was already clear to Anthony that the kindest treatment for Patch would be to put him to sleep, gently and painlessly, and when Holly examined the old dog she agreed. She diagnosed the lump on his side as a hernia, caused by him straining to go to the toilet, which had become almost impossible because of the angry, ulcerated tumour on his bottom.

As she examined the mass, she could see that the lymph nodes around it were enlarged, an indication that the cancer had spread to other areas of his body. Even an exploratory operation to find out exactly where the cancer had spread to would be too much of an ordeal for an elderly dog in such a debilitated condition. With so little chance of recovery from the operation and any further treatment, it wouldn't be fair to put him through it.

In an attempt to tackle Patch's flea problem, his owner had shaved the poor dog's body apart from his ears. The only effect it had had was that the fleas had migrated to those last remaining clumps of fur. On further examination, there seemed to be a small black mass in each ear, but when touched the mass broke up as fleas scattered in every direction. It was appalling to see, and difficult to imagine the torture it must have been causing the dog.

Sadly for Patch, his life was over, but at least Holly was able to end it with dignity. For this particular animal there was no pleasure at all left in his world, which for many months had been dominated by pain, torment and darkness. For Anthony, his greatest sadness was that he hadn't been called in twelve months earlier, when there would have been a chance to at least give Patch a few comfortable months at the end of his life. He sighed with relief, however, when the old fella was eased out of his misery.

'When a dog has to be put down, I don't find it easy to get

away from the sadness. But in this case I didn't have one ounce of regret. I knew what Holly would decide before I took him in. I'm so glad he had a pain-free end, which was all we could give him, but so much better than the hell he'd been living.'

Socks' fate wasn't wholly certain at that stage either, but Holly agreed with Anthony that there was some hope and therefore his life was worth fighting for. The owner had told Anthony he'd only had Socks for a short time, having taken him in as a favour to someone else who still owned him. However, much later, when he was formally interviewed by the RSPCA, he admitted the dog had been living with him for well over six months – plenty of time for him to have got help treating him.

As Holly handled him, Socks kept his tail tight between his legs and shivered in fear. He was promptly given antibiotics, steroids and painkillers, and a medicated bath, as well as a much-needed mani-pedi, so that his curled claws were reduced to a normal length.

Holly's main concern was Socks' ears, however, which were infected right down his ear canals. The thickened skin, caused by his incessant scratching, ran right down them too, making him practically deaf. Sometimes, when an infection as a result of a flea infestation or mange is so acute and cannot be controlled, and the dog's ears are blocked with infection, no amount of treatment will work. Holly held out hope for Socks, though, and a regime of ear drops was started. The poor dog cried with pain as they were put in, but submitted to the treatment without cowering away.

'Any human who has ever had an ear problem knows how toe-curlingly painful it is,' acknowledges Anthony. 'It's close to unbearable, and as humans we go straight for treatment. Ear problems are so common in neglected dogs, and the pain must be excruciating — they can do nothing except rely on their owner for help. A dog can't take himself to the vet.'

Socks was a much younger dog than Patch — an estimated eighteen months old, though his denuded body made him look older — with a better immune system and a stronger chance of fighting off the serious infection. Although his flea infestation was one of the worst Holly had ever seen, she felt there was a chance it was fixable, and started treatment for it straight away. Medicated baths and the use of a specially formulated flea shampoo were the order of the day.

'Usually, with an animal infested with fleas, all we see is flea dirt,' Holly explained. Flea faeces look like small, pepper-like specks, round in shape. 'In this case, we can see the fleas crawling on his body, which means there must be a massive infestation in the place he's come from.'

Both dogs were underweight when they were rescued, and had also suffered long-term incarceration in the squalid house. Had the owner taken them out at any point, alarmed members of the public would certainly have told him to get them both to a vet, and probably rung the RSPCA them-selves. So it was clear they had been kept out of sight in the home. The state of Socks' claws proved he hadn't walked properly for months.

The owner's version of events was that he didn't take the dogs out because he'd been involved in a fracas in the street outside his home some time earlier, during which Socks had been stabbed in the back and had to be rushed to a vet for emergency treatment. Anthony checked out the story, which was true. However, he also found out that the RSPCA had footed the bill for the emergency treatment, which made it harder to accept that the owner had never taken either of his suffering dogs for treatment again, especially as the vet was so close at hand.

'He knew that there was help available. It's never a matter of money, because no vet should turn away an animal in an emergency, and there are charities that will meet the bill. For non-emergencies the PDSA is there to help. It is heartbreaking and inexcusable to let two dogs get into the state Patch and Socks were in.'

The owner was successfully prosecuted, given a four-month suspended prison sentence and banned for life from keeping animals. In court, he was visibly upset as he stood in the dock, but that was small consolation for the RSPCA team involved.

After giving Socks his initial treatment, Holly told Anthony that he was going to need a lot of TLC over the next few months, and although it was by no means certain that all his fur would grow back, he would definitely survive.

Care is exactly what Socks got at the RSPCA Wirral & Chester Branch's Animal Centre. When Anthony transferred Socks there on that first night following his rescue, he sat with the agitated dog in the kennel for a few minutes. He didn't want to leave, knowing that although Socks was in a better place, he was still feeling wretched and his new surroundings were strange and unfamiliar. Even though Socks had been acutely neglected over a long period of time, the filthy flat where he had lived with his companion Patch and their owner was possibly the only home he had known. Leaving it was obviously a wrench, especially as he was now spending his first night alone, possibly for the first time in his whole life. Before the painkillers kicked in, it must have seemed to poor Socks that his situation had gone from bad to worse. When animals have chronic conditions it can be days or weeks before they start to feel fully comfortable.

As he does with all his rescued dogs, Anthony made a

point of calling in to see Socks whenever he went to the centre, and he loved to give him some play and attention, sometimes dealing with his admin sitting on the floor of Socks' run, just keeping the dog company. On his days off, he'd pop by to spend ten minutes with him, giving him a treat. Anthony knew that a major part of Socks' rehabilitation would be meeting friendly, caring people, to renew his trust in the human race. By beginning to establish healthy relationships, Socks would stand a better chance of finding a new home for life.

In the end, it didn't take long for Socks to start feeling better and settle into his new, pain-free life. With the constant itching gone, the open sores where he'd scratched himself raw began to scab over. His ears no longer caused him agony and, to the delight of all the staff, his fur began to grow back. For Anthony, the biggest thrill was seeing Socks' tail, which had been tucked between his legs in fear, wagging delightedly.

After five weeks of intensive treatment and attention, Socks' transformation was unbelievable. His new coat of fur was coming through, a glossy black with a white flash down his chest. He loved going for walks with the centre volunteers, and when Anthony took him out into the centre's paddock, the little fella romped around the obstacle course like any other normal, healthy, energetic dog. Anthony could see that Socks would make a loving family pet, and all he hoped for now was that the right new owners would come forward for a dog that had endured such a terrible early life.

That's where Wendy Ehlen and her young son, Max, enter the story.

Wendy had been left distraught by the death of her old dog a few months previously, a Staffie-Westie cross called Eddie, who for thirteen years had been a beloved and loving pet. She'd got him from the RSPCA Wirral & Chester Branch Animal Centre, where his mother had died giving birth, so he'd been with Wendy for his entire life. His death hit her so hard that she swore she couldn't go through the loss of a pet again. She vowed that there would be no more dogs.

Though, as is often the case, the house felt empty without an animal. When you're used to having one around, suddenly the space seems too large, and the quiet becomes unbearable. One day, browsing online, Wendy saw Socks' profile on the RSPCA's website, and there was something about his eyes that singled him out from other dogs whose stories came up. It was, she says, love at first sight, and she wanted to see him.

She went to the animal centre with her then husband, Shayne. Socks wasn't exactly handsome: he still had fur missing from his chest and around his ears, and his bottom was bald. Although his claws had been cut back, years of neglect meant that they now grew crookedly, making his feet look misshapen. He was happy to take a few biscuits from Wendy and Shayne, though, and despite being a bit taken aback by his size — he was so much bigger than her wee Eddie had been — her instant feeling of love for him did not waver.

It was crucial, of course, that Max, who was five and a half at the time, met Socks before he could be adopted. As far as everyone knew, Socks had no experience with children, and if he and Max didn't bond it would be the end of that particular dream. Socks wouldn't be the dog for them.

Fortunately, the plucky dog immediately took to his new young friend, and the pair spent a very happy half-hour together, Max throwing a ball for him, and Socks tirelessly chasing around the field to retrieve it. It was clear to everyone watching that the relationship was off to a good start, and that meant Socks had found his forever home. The staff

decided that, even though he was still on a treatment programme, it would be better for Socks to be at home with his
new family as soon as possible, with Wendy keeping up the
regime of ear drops, steroids and medicated baths that he
needed.

Wendy didn't tell Max that she was bringing Socks home
on the day she collected him from the animal centre, just in
case anything held the adoption up. When they got home,
Max was still at school and she lay on the couch with Socks,
cradling him like a baby. It was a special moment between
them, something Wendy will never forget. As Socks looked
up at her it was as if he was saying, 'I'm safe, I trust you.'
Wendy's heart melted with love for him.

The first thing Wendy did was rename him. The name
Socks was, she believed, associated with his miserable early
life and she was determined to give him a completely fresh
start. It was Max who chose the name Buddy, because he
instantly saw the new dog in his life as his best friend. However, if they had the chance to name him again, they'd go
with Shadow.

'That's because he shadows us all the time, sticking by us,'
Wendy explains. 'Even if I'm having a bath, he's in the bathroom, lying down next to the tub. It's as if he has to have one
of us in his sight at all times, to make sure his new life doesn't
end.' In those early days, Buddy's neck was a livid pink and
he couldn't bear it being touched. His ears and the back of his
head were also very tender, as were his paws, and Wendy
had to be very careful when she bathed him every day. Even
though it hurt, he let her do it, as if he knew she would never
do anything to harm him and was doing it for his own good.

Now that Wendy has had him for more than two years,
Buddy only needs the medicated baths occasionally. He'll
need ear drops for the rest of his life, however, and although

the steroids have been cut from four tablets to one a day, whenever Wendy has tried to stop them completely his skin condition has flared up again. The staff at the animal centre advised her that Buddy had a very sensitive stomach, and they'd found only one brand of tinned food that he could tolerate. It's probable that his skin problems are caused by food allergies, so Wendy now only feeds him a hypoallergenic dry dog food.

Buddy's fur has largely grown back, but his tummy and underarms are still bald, and these are the first areas to itch if his skin condition returns. When Wendy sees him dragging himself across the carpet on his tummy in order to relieve the itch, she knows it's time to up his steroid medication again. He hates going to the vet so much that Wendy bought a pair of clippers, and now clips his claws herself. The level of care and attention she gives him is in stark contrast to Buddy's previous life.

Wendy wasn't told much about his history, apart from the fact that he'd been rescued with another dog that had to be put down, but she soon became familiar with his battle scars. Every time she cuddled him, she felt another part of his history under her hand, such as the train track of stitches down his back from the stabbing. He also has a slit in his tongue, which Wendy guesses is the result of him licking food directly from a tin with a razor-sharp edge, and one of his front teeth is missing. Whenever she found another reminder of his terrible past, Wendy would fuss him and tears would spring to her eyes at the thought of anyone being cruel to such a lovely, trusting creature.

When Wendy and Shayne first settled down together, they agreed they wanted a dog, having both been around dogs when they were growing up. When Wendy was a child, the family had a white-and-black dog of indeterminate breed, which had followed her mum home one day and sat on the doorstep until allowed inside. Enquiries failed to find his owner, so he was called Lucky — because it was his lucky day when he followed her home and became a much-loved family pet. They already had a Labrador-German shepherd cross by the name of Tina and, at one point, Wendy's mum was feeding a total of thirteen stray cats who were in need of some extra nutrition and must have spread the word there was a free feast available. Even today, she still feeds one, nicknamed Pug, who turns up regularly from who knows where.

When Wendy and Shayne married, they didn't want children initially, and Eddie was their 'furry baby'. So, when Max was born, it's unsurprising that Eddie found it hard to adjust, and although Max adored the dog the affection was not reciprocated. That was why it was so wonderful for Wendy to find that Buddy was as devoted to Max as Max was to him. The minute Max gets home from school each day, he shouts out, 'Where's my Buddy Boo?' and the inseparable pair roll around on the floor together.

Buddy is also devoted to Wendy's parents. Every day, her dad takes him to his allotment, which is ninety feet long and where Buddy loves to play in the mud, coming back filthy without fail. However, it was on one trip to the allotment that Buddy nearly lost his life, an incident that reduced Wendy to a distraught wreck.

At the plot, there is a twelve-foot trampoline where Max and Buddy love bouncing together. Wendy's dad was amusing Buddy by throwing him a heavy rubber ball, and the dog ran under the trampoline with it, refusing to come out. When he eventually did, it was with the much-diminished, chewed-up remains of the ball. Nobody thought any more of it, assuming that the rest of the ball was still under the trampoline, and that Buddy had simple mauled it to shreds. However, six hours later, the normally lively Buddy grew listless and still, and then began to shake violently.

Wendy rushed him to the vet's, and an X-ray showed a piece of the ball trapped in his bowel. An emergency operation followed and three large, pebble-sized pieces of rubber were removed from his intestine. While he was in the operating theatre, Wendy was beside herself, convinced that he was going to die, and the only consolation she could think of was that they'd given him several months of happiness after a terrible start in life. She knew that he'd had lots of love and that at least he hadn't died in that 'horrible house'. Luckily for all of them, Buddy made a good recovery, and within a couple of days was back at home with the family.

Perhaps because he'd only ever lived in a flat before, Buddy didn't seem to understand the concept of stairs when he first moved in with Wendy and Shayne. For about a month, he just lay at the bottom of the stairs when they went off to bed, not making any sound but clearly longing to go up after them. Step by step, he gradually moved up, until one night a few weeks later he appeared on the landing, looking around the door into their bedroom. He didn't need to be called in twice: at the first invitation he was up on the bed, under the covers, snuggling into Wendy's back, and he has slept on the bed ever since.

The biggest love in Buddy's new life is clearly his family, but food comes a close second. Perhaps because he was underweight when he was rescued, he is obsessed with filling his belly, which can be a problem because of his allergies — whether it's a tummy upset from eating too quickly, or getting his paws on something he's allergic to, which then sets off his itching. It also causes mayhem in the household.

Eddie was a small dog, so for thirteen years Wendy never

had to worry about food left on the kitchen counter. It was a learning curve when she adopted a dog who can stand on his hind legs and snaffle anything in reach. Wendy first realized that Buddy was a food thief when she cooked a full Sunday lunch, then couldn't find the twelve Yorkshire puddings she'd made. Buddy had eaten each and every one of them. Another time, Shayne left an uncooked pizza on the worktop while the oven heated up, and came back to find Buddy had scoffed it raw.

Then there was the time they were living with Wendy's parents and Wendy's mum won an array of prizes at a tea dance. She'd left the bag containing her winnings on the floor unbeknown to Wendy, who then popped out to collect Max from school, a round trip that takes a mere fifteen minutes. On her return Wendy thought the house had been broken into. There was a trail of packaging and wrappers strewn everywhere. Buddy had eaten a whole panettone, two packets of biscuits, a gingerbread house, a Madeira cake and a giant tube of Smarties.

On days like that, after a swift call to the vet, Buddy has to have extra steroids to ward off an allergic reaction, just as he does if Max sometimes sneaks part of his meal to his mate, or if he steals Max's food when Max is too preoccupied watching a cartoon on television to notice. Wendy can't bring herself to tell either of them off.

Sometimes Buddy manages to cause havoc without actually eating anything. When it was Wendy's mum's turn to provide the tea and coffee for another tea dance, she left a shopping bag filled with various goodies ready to take. In it there was a bag of sugar. Attracted by the smell, Buddy took the packet out of the shopping bag, ripped it open and dragged it through the house – leaving a kilo of sugar in his wake. When Wendy and Max walked in, they went into panic mode.

'If Nanny finds out, she'll go mental,' Wendy told Max. 'You've got to help me; they're due back any minute.'

She grabbed the vacuum cleaner while Max scooped the sugar up with the coal shovel. But where to put the sugar? Wendy knew if it went into the bin, her mother would spot it. So Wendy and Max went into the garden and sprinkled it over the lawn, as if they were sowing grass seed. Then, Wendy nipped out quickly to buy a replacement and Buddy lived to see another day . . .

While they were living at her parents' house, Buddy also discovered he could open the fridge, where he promptly devoured some green beans and lettuce. He also made short work of a punnet of tomatoes collected from the allotment. However, perhaps his greatest crime was when the family was having a large get-together and Wendy bought a giant tower of profiteroles as a centrepiece for the table. She went upstairs to change for the event, unaware that Buddy had sussed out how to open the latch on the door to the dining room. He'd scoffed half the profiteroles by the time she got back downstairs, resulting in another panicked call to the vet.

Wendy has tried hard to train him out of his food obsession, but believes it is hardwired into him from his early life. The only solution is to be constantly vigilant, or else accept that you'll be constantly disappointed.

Wendy has also needed help from an animal behaviour expert to improve Buddy's social skills. Although he's the happiest, most loving dog you could meet when in the family home, he's naturally suspicious of strangers and not at all happy with the dogs he meets outside the house. After the attack and stabbing, it's understandable that he's wary of people he doesn't know, but he's getting better and Wendy is hopeful that, with encouragement and training, he'll learn to be as easy-going when out and about as he is at home.

'He's a very needy boy, making up for his start in life with all the love and stroking he can get. If Max comes into my bed, we play a game with Buddy. He lies between us and we both stroke him, then I count "one, two, three" and we both stop at the same moment. Buddy whimpers until we start again. He's our lovely boy.'

TIPS ON HOW TO CARE FOR YOUR DOG

Puppies

THE FIRST fourteen weeks of a puppy's life are vital for their development — this is the 'socialization period', the time when they learn the most information about the characteristics of dogs, other animals and humans they come into contact with. Their experiences during this period shape their personality and behaviour as an adult dog — puppies who have had positive experiences of lots of different types of people are less likely to be wary when you handle and approach them, and are more likely to grow up to be friendly and happy in the company of people and other animals. This helps them take new or unusual situations in their stride, which is better for their stress levels, and those of their owners! Puppies that have had a lack of social contact during this period are more at risk of behaviours associated with fear and/or anxiety later in life.

Puppies also need to be introduced gradually to a wide range of everyday household sounds and objects that they'll encounter in their new homes, such as vacuum cleaners, so that they learn not to be afraid of them. This gentle exposure will give them the best chance of growing into a happy and healthy adult, and able to cope well with a home life.

▶

It's also important that the gradual, positive introduction to new people, animals and situations is continued throughout their lives, with owners taking their puppy, or new adult dog, to training classes. Training your dog is not only a part of responsible dog ownership, it also provides important mental stimulation for your dog, and is a great way to get to know each other. Training classes help you understand how your dog learns, and provide opportunities for your dog to develop important social skills. Training should always be a positive experience for dogs and should be reward-based, with food, play or toys. Don't join any class where the training techniques rely on fear, pain, choke chains, shouting or hitting.

For more information visit www.rspca.org.uk/dogtrainer.

CHAPTER 12

Ruby

SHE WAS so tiny you could hold her in one hand. She
weighed about the same as a bag of sugar, and was the
smallest puppy you've ever set eyes on – a pug crossed with a
shih-tzu – and no more than eight weeks old.

However, when Inspector Anthony Joynes first saw the
little bundle of fur, she was screaming in pain, huddled into
a corner of her kennel, terrified if anyone came near her. She
had clearly been the victim of a savage attack. For Anthony,
it was the start of a long battle to get the brute who had
attacked the little puppy into jail, and it was also the first day

of the struggle to repair the terrible damage that had been inflicted on the tiny dog.

The puppy was brought into the CVets surgery by a young woman and her sister. The pup was clearly in such pain that she was rushed through to vet Gemma Davidson ahead of all the other animals waiting to be seen. According to the young woman, the little dog had suffered its injuries when her boyfriend, who was the owner of the dog, was on his own with her; he claimed she'd fallen off the bed and hurt herself as she hit the floor.

However, the vet knew immediately that it would have taken great force to inflict this degree of injury to the pup's jaw. She couldn't close her mouth, she couldn't eat, she wouldn't allow anyone to touch her head, and when she was picked up she screamed, a terrible piercing shriek filled with pain and terror. This had been no accident.

Veterinary nurse Lauren Harrison helped the vet put an anaesthetic line into the whimpering bundle so that she could be X-rayed. The results were truly shocking. The left side of her lower jaw was not just broken, the bone was shattered, with slivers having slid away down the side of the jaw. This was a massive injury, not something that could have been caused by falling off a bed. Very young animals have soft, flexible bones, designed to withstand simple accidents: this injury had been inflicted upon the tiny pup with huge force. In addition to her shattered jaw, she also had a hairline fracture of her skull.

A call went out to Anthony: it was clear someone was responsible for causing this little one such a terrible trauma. When he arrived at the surgery and saw the sad little puppy, he rang the police immediately, and they came to the practice to formally seize the pup as evidence, and put her into his care.

She was called Babs, according to the woman who had

brought her in, but straight away the surgery staff wanted to give her a new name for what they hoped would be her new life. Re-naming is always a symbolic act. Nurse Lauren, who had fallen in love with the puppy at first sight, re-named her Ruby, and the rest of the staff agreed that it suited her. However, the vet warned that it was touch and go as to whether Ruby would recover from her injuries; it was perhaps unwise to get too close to her. The damage done to her jaw was so severe, and she was so small, that it would be a very tricky operation to fix it. If she wasn't able to eat normally again, then the kindest option would be to put her down.

That day, she was just too poorly to undergo the operation. She was unable to walk properly, and at first vet Gemma feared she also had spinal injuries. However, when nothing showed on the X-ray, it was decided the swelling on her brain was affecting her movement, and she needed rest and care until it subsided. She was given intravenous painkillers, which at least brought her some respite from the agony she was in, and she was fed every two hours with a liquid recovery food, which was put on her tongue so that she could swallow it.

She needed round-the-clock care, and Lauren volunteered for the job, taking little Ruby home with her that night. At the time, Lauren lived with her mother, Pamela, and sister, Alana, and she rang her mum to ask if it was all right to bring a sick puppy home. Pamela said no at first, because she was determined not to get too attached to another dog, having recently lost the last in a long line of King Charles spaniels and shih-tzus. She was so upset when their last pet died that, like many owners, she said 'never again', but Lauren knew that if her mum saw little Ruby, she would be as besotted with her as everyone at the vet practice was. And after all, it was just for a night or two . . .

'Do you mind picking me up tonight as I'll be working late?' Lauren asked her mum. Her ruse worked, of course, because when Pamela turned up to take her daughter home and saw Ruby, she fell in love with the sad little ball of fur and was very happy to take her with them. How could she not? She went from 'no' to 'can I cuddle her?' in a couple of seconds – which Lauren, knowing her mum, was sure would be the case.

Throughout the night, and for the following night as well, Lauren woke every two hours to give Ruby her painkillers and her liquid food. She didn't really sleep, knowing how much the little dog was depending on her. Ruby was in a crate in Lauren's bedroom, to keep her secure and to stop her from moving around too much. As the painkillers began to take effect, her affectionate and trusting personality quickly began to shine through.

Lauren has always loved animals and knew from an early age that she wanted to work with them. After leaving school, she started working as a volunteer at the veterinary practice to see if she enjoyed it. From the first day she loved it, and after working full time as a helper at first, she started training as a veterinary nurse. She'd seen many suffering animals, but Ruby's case was the worst. The screams from such a tiny creature really got to her.

'Sometimes an animal is brought in after an accident, and the owner is there, distraught. But this owner seemed to be the person who did it, which made it all the more terrible,' she said.

On the third day of Ruby's recovery, head vet Nick Whieldon, who undertakes the orthopaedic operations at the surgery, felt Ruby was strong enough to be operated on. It was going to be a very delicate procedure.

The three usual options for such an injury – putting an external frame on the jaw to hold the bones together, inserting tiny metal plates inside, or wiring the bones together – would be difficult to do on such a tiny dog. Although Ruby's size was against her in this way, the fact that she was so very young worked in her favour, because her bones were soft and still growing rapidly. Young bones repair quickly; older bones take much longer. So Nick decided to improvise with strong suture material, used to stitch together injuries. He drilled three holes into the jaw bone and pieced it back together with reasonable stability, then stitched up the wound with the suture material. The whole operation took two agonizing hours, and everyone at the surgery who had come into contact with brave little Ruby crossed their fingers for the duration, hoping that she would pull through OK, and that her jaw would heal. For Lauren, it was a particularly difficult time. She had to put her professional head on to assist during the operation, and try hard not to think about Ruby as her own special girl.

Nick knew that the stitches would last; they could do so, sometimes for as long as six months. He also knew that Ruby's bones were growing fast, and that she would heal quickly. Young animals are healing machines, and bone fractures can repair themselves in as little as four weeks, so it was likely the stitches would outlive the healing process. That's what Nick was counting on.

That night, Ruby went home with Lauren as usual. She'd made it through the operation. Still sleepy from the anaesthetic, she wobbled adorably when she staggered to her feet and licked Lauren's hand, her tail wagging more slowly than usual, as if she were summoning the strength to show her happiness.

For the next two weeks, Lauren continued to get up every night to administer painkillers and small amounts of food. To her great delight, Ruby soon began to walk normally again. Vet Nick was keeping a close eye on her when Lauren brought her in to work each day, and he was delighted to see that after as little as two weeks, her jaw was almost completely healed. Most importantly, she was able to start eating without help.

Lauren and her family had moved house only a week or two before Lauren first brought Ruby home, and a week later it was Christmas, a celebration that was dominated by Ruby's two-hourly feeds. And yet there were no complaints. 'She was the best Christmas present everyone in our family could have wished for,' Lauren said.

From the beginning of Ruby's life-saving treatment, Anthony began his investigation into what had happened to the puppy, and who was responsible. For him, cases don't get any worse than this. To see a defenceless puppy having been beaten, when it's completely reliant on the person responsible for it, is the lowest point of the job, he says. It fires him up, though, and makes him want to bring the sort of callous brute who can do this to justice.

The first step was to interview the young woman who, with her sister, had brought the puppy in. He heard that her partner – who was now very definitely her ex-partner – had phoned her when she was at work to say the dog had fallen off the bed. When she got home, she had found the puppy in great pain, with a horribly swollen face. Whenever her boyfriend Gary – not his real name – went near the little pup, she'd screamed and whimpered. The woman had been very worried, as she couldn't get the puppy to eat. She'd spent the night trying to give her fluids. The following morning she'd taken her to the vet's.

She told Anthony that she was suspicious of her partner, because the puppy was clearly terrified of him. Gary had once thrown a plate at the woman, so she knew he had a violent temper. Gradually, more stories of his animal cruelty emerged. On a previous occasion, when the woman had had a row with him about her going to a party without him, she'd come back to find a puppy Gary owned lying in its crate, lifeless and bleeding from the nose. Convinced he'd inflicted the damage, her family paid for a post-mortem, but the results were inconclusive. Anthony, however, is in no doubt, because puppies don't mortally injure themselves in their crate. There has to have been another party involved.

The woman also told Anthony that Gary used to buy rabbits from a pet store chain, but the rabbits never survived for long. Anthony was able to check with the store in question, which, unlike some pet shops, is meticulous about recording the names of people who buy animals. Gary had purchased six rabbits over a period of seven months, and none had survived.

Worryingly, she also told him the story of Lary, a cat Gary had taken on from an ex-partner of his only seven weeks previously. Forty-eight hours after Lary moved in with them, the woman received a phone call at work to say that the cat had injured itself. According to Gary, the cat had hidden behind the fridge – presumably in fear – and he'd yanked it out by its back end, causing enough damage, physical and psychological, for it to become incontinent. As it was covered in faeces, he placed it in the shower and turned on the water – cruel and unnatural treatment for a cat. When the woman got home, she had found Lary collapsed and limp on the bed, still soaking wet, one of her eyes red and unable to move her legs. The cat died that night, probably in great agony and misery, and the woman's partner disposed of the body.

Anthony went to interview Gary. After everything he'd heard about the man's treatment of animals, he needed to suppress his natural anger, and behave professionally. It wasn't easy. The man lived in a caravan at a site where new caravans were stored before being sold. He was given accommodation in return for working as the site security guard. He was also a personal trainer, and ran some training classes in strength conditioning for the police. Anthony knew he was therefore strong and fit. The kind of damage Anthony had seen inflicted was likely the work of a bully or a sadistic psychopath. Either way, it was intolerable and criminal. Anthony wanted to see justice done.

Gary wasn't at the caravan when Anthony arrived, or perhaps he chose not to open the door. Anthony left his card and it wasn't long before the man rang him. He was very cool, calm and collected, and maintained that his spiteful girlfriend, who had of course now dumped him, was out to make trouble for him. Anthony was used to malicious allegations, often made when relationships have broken up, but he was convinced that the amount of detail the girlfriend had given him was too much to be a pack of lies. He couldn't ignore it, and besides, there was the overwhelming evidence of poor little Ruby's injuries.

Gary persisted, though, addressing Anthony in a matey way. He insisted that, like Anthony, he was an animal lover and would assist Anthony's inquiries in any way he could. Anthony made an appointment to go back to the caravan to see him in person, but shortly before he was due, Gary rang and said he'd been called away to a family emergency in Leicestershire. Nonetheless, Anthony went back to the caravan site, accompanied by two police officers.

When they arrived, there was no answer at the door, but it was clear Gary was either there or had been there until very recently. It was a very cold December day, and all the unoccupied caravans' windows were glazed with ice. But not Gary's. The windows were fogged up with condensation, showing there was heating on inside, and that it was likely occupied. Anthony had a look round, and in an outhouse he found a cat litter tray and a supply of cat litter.

As their knocks went unanswered, Anthony and the two officers left the site. Within five minutes, the man rang Anthony to say that he'd been there at the caravan all along, and that his family emergency had been called off. Anthony and the policemen returned, the man was arrested on suspicion of animal welfare offences and, without resisting, was taken to the police station.

Anthony and one of the police officers formally interviewed him. He was still calm and collected, but not quite as relaxed as he'd originally been on the phone, nor as confident. He was still maintaining there was nothing in the allegations made by his former partner. He claimed he'd only ever bought one rabbit, until he came up against the evidence from the pet store chain. He denied all knowledge of ever having a cat when questioned about Lary, until faced with the evidence of the cat litter tray. At this point he admitted that there had been an incident, but claimed he was blameless and the cat had injured itself.

As for poor Ruby, after originally saying she'd fallen off the bed, the man now admitted that he'd swiped her with the back of his hand when she'd bitten him. With the information he had from the vet about the amount of force needed to inflict Ruby's injury, Anthony knew the man was still trying to play down his attack on the puppy. Even quite a strong backhand wouldn't have been enough to cause the awful damage Anthony had seen.

He was also disgusted that a man who prided himself on his physical fitness could have been so distressed — even if the little puppy had mouthed him, the way puppies do — that he'd reacted so violently. There were, it was noted, no marks on his hand, no evidence of him having been bitten.

It was an interview in which the perpetrator tied himself up in knots with his own lies, and Anthony felt confident he had enough evidence for a prosecution. However, it was at the end of the interview that the bombshell dropped.

'Have you ever been in trouble with the police before? Have you ever been in prison?' the police officer asked.

Gary visibly crumbled, put his head in his hands and said, very quietly, 'Yeah, yeah.'

He told them that twelve years earlier he had been sentenced to seven years in jail for the manslaughter of his two-year-old son. When he was released after serving half his sentence, he changed his name and eventually established himself as a personal trainer in the North West.

When Anthony heard about this previous conviction, he was shocked – though not as much as a less experienced animal cruelty expert might have been. In all his years in the job, when dealing with non-accidental injuries, he has found that the perpetrators are almost always young men, and that they either already have, or go on to have, convictions for violence towards partners or children, or both. Time and time again, his experience has shown there to be a direct correlation between domestic violence and animal cruelty.*

---

* The links between offenders who abuse animals and those who abuse children or partners is well known to RSPCA inspectors, and they work closely with other agencies, often contacting the NSPCC when their investigation into a neglected or abused animal leaves them with concerns for children living in the same home.

A survey of all referrals made by the RSPCA to the NSPCC showed that in 50 per cent of all these families action was taken, with 80 per cent being investigated for neglect and 20 per cent for physical abuse. The other 50 per cent were families already on the radar, where the relevant agencies, usually social services, were supervising and managing the risks to the children.

Despite his history, Gary still pleaded not guilty when charged with animal cruelty, much to Anthony's disdain. In his eyes, people like Gary should hold their hands up, admit their guilt, apologize and face up to their punishment. However, at the last minute, just before the case reached the courtroom, Gary changed his plea to guilty, probably having been given legal advice. He pleaded guilty to animal cruelty in the death of Lary the cat and the injuries to Ruby (or Babs), the little pug. A date was set for him to appear at Wirral Magistrates' Court, in front of a district judge, for sentencing.

On the appointed date, Anthony went to court full of expectation. He wanted to see justice done but instead he found himself walking out in frustration. Gary had jumped bail and failed to appear, unwilling to face justice. It was now out of Anthony's hands. The police put out a warrant for Gary's arrest, but he had disappeared from the area, and for a time Anthony felt despondent that he had successfully evaded justice.

Most academic research into the link between domestic violence and animal cruelty has been done in the United States, where a study by police in Chicago showed that 65 per cent of people arrested for animal abuse had previously been arrested for a physical attack on another person. Pet abuse is now regarded as one of the four main predictors of domestic violence and child abuse for most US police forces.

More than four out of every five women who fled to domestic violence shelters to avoid abuse reported that their partners also abused or had killed the family pet. An even higher number of families under supervision for abuse of children were found to have animal abuse in the household.

As one expert said, 'Animal cruelty is one of the earliest and most dramatic indicators that an individual is developing a pattern of seeking power and control through the abuse of others. When animals in a home are abused or neglected, it is a warning sign that others in the household may be in danger.'

However, through some clever detection work by the police, Gary was traced to London, where he had once again changed his name and set up another business as a personal trainer. He unwittingly agreed to a session with a client who turned out to be a policeman from Merseyside, and at the same time the Metropolitan Police arrived to arrest him. He was transported back to the Wirral for the sentencing hearing.

Out of the country on holiday at the time, Anthony missed the court appearance at which the vicious brute who did so much damage to Ruby was given the longest possible custodial sentence for animal cruelty: six months in prison. He was also banned from keeping animals for life, ordered to pay £2,423 in court costs and, after completing his sentence, he would have to undergo a twelve-month probation supervision. It was the maximum possible sentence.

Anthony heard about the sentence in a message from a colleague, and was disappointed that he hadn't been able to be there to see this man face justice.

'There are three highlights of this job for me. The first is when I see a nervous or aggressive dog, which has known nothing but unhappiness, open up and show love, affection and trust. That's a magic moment. The second is when I see an animal settled with a new family, with a happy life ahead of them. The third is the moment I see the perpetrators sentenced in court. When I've worked hard on a cruelty case, and sometimes been treated with scorn by people who think they're above the law, scoffing at me as if to say, "You've got nothing on me", then I like to see them in the dock, and that's when I know I've secured justice for the poor animal they mistreated. So I would've liked to see him in handcuffs being led from the dock to go to prison. But even if I wasn't there, it was a great victory.'

In court, the judge said, 'The facts of this case have

chilling echoes of the attack on his child, which led to his death. I think you are an extremely dangerous man. In the context of this case you are one of the most dangerous men in relation to animals I have ever come across.'

Referring to the guilty man's flight to London, the judge continued, 'I believe quite simply that you did not want to face justice. It was only through luck and good police work they tracked you down.'

Anthony was not the only person who was pleased to see the man who hurt Ruby so badly put back into prison. The mother of the little boy who died said she wasn't shocked at the violence. She also complained about the length of sentence the boy's father got. In her opinion it was far too light.

After his conviction for animal cruelty, she said, 'This case shows that I was right all along. He should have had a longer sentence. People like this often go on to reoffend. I am worried that he can change his name, and people in the area won't know what he has done.'

It is a fear that occasionally crosses Anthony's mind, knowing that this man with an uncontrollably violent temper and a perverted interest in inflicting cruelty on small, defenceless creatures is now out of prison, and could have changed his name yet again and be living in another area of the country. Mercifully, it's a thought that is very far from Ruby's mind. She's now fully grown − though still small − a bundle of energy, and happy and trusting, living very contentedly with Lauren.

Anthony believes the pair are soulmates, made for each other. 'She's an adorable little thing, and she's found an owner who gives her all the love she needs. Hopefully her cruel beginning has dropped from her memory.'

Ruby's jaw is slightly deformed, and sometimes one of the teeth in her lower jaw protrudes above her lip, but she's able to eat more or less normally, favouring chewing on one side of her jaw. She occasionally has seizures, during which she goes very quiet and puts her head and front paws on the floor with her bottom up in the air, as if she is praying. Her eyes flicker, then, after a couple of minutes she recovers but remains very agitated for a couple of hours, then she sleeps deeply for the rest of the day. As the seizures only happen about once a month, she's not being treated for them, but her condition is being closely monitored.

'Nobody could say for certain that the fits are the result of the head trauma, as lots of dogs have epilepsy anyway,' says vet Nick. 'But if you have a knock to the brain, as Ruby did, it can induce fits. We would only give medication if they were more severe and happening much more frequently.'

Lauren takes it all in her stride. She knew from the moment she saw Ruby that she wanted to keep her, but the puppy was such a delightful little character that one of the police officers involved with the case and two other members of staff at the practice also offered her a permanent home. Lauren was the lucky one, though, and after her sleepless nights feeding Ruby to keep her alive in the early days, it seemed only right that she should be the one to adopt her. Since then, Ruby's become a fully fledged member of the Harrison family, sleeping on Lauren's bed every night.

'From the moment I first saw her sad eyes, I just wanted to give her a good life, to make up for what had happened to her.'

Because she was so poorly in the early weeks of her life, little Ruby couldn't have her routine vaccinations until she was five months old. Puppies shouldn't go outside and mix with other dogs until they are vaccinated against infectious diseases including distemper, parvovirus and kennel cough, so usually this means they have restricted access outdoors for the first six to eight weeks of their lives. However, because this had to be much longer in Ruby's case, it meant she missed out on early contact with other pets. Lauren was a bit worried that it would be difficult socializing Ruby with other dogs as a result. She needn't have been concerned, though, as despite being a bit nervous on her first few trips into the big wide world, Ruby's natural exuberance soon took over, and she now welcomes everybody, human or canine, with a wagging tail and a friendly lick.

Unlike many dogs, there's nothing Ruby likes better than having a bath and being groomed. The minute Lauren gets out the hairdryer to blow-dry her own hair, Ruby sits looking at her expectantly, as if to say, 'When's it my turn?'

Since she adopted Ruby, Lauren has left her mum's home to live with her boyfriend, Tolga. Together they've adopted another rescue dog, a German shepherd called Thea, who is at the opposite end of the size scale to Ruby. The two get on very well and are inseparable, sleeping together during the day and playing together – although at night, Ruby still insists on snuggling under the covers with Lauren. She hates getting up in the morning, and when Lauren tries to rouse her she digs deeper under the duvet.

Ruby still goes to work with Lauren every day, happily treating the staff room at the surgery as her second home. She doesn't bother with the dog beds in the room, preferring to sit on the table where everyone who comes in can see her and make a fuss. She clearly sees herself as the practice mascot.

'I'm very lucky to have her,' admits Lauren. 'I hate to think about what happened to her, but I am so glad that she came to me. Nick is a miracle-worker; he gave her back her life.'

TIPS ON HOW TO CARE FOR YOUR DOG

Body language

JUST LIKE us, dogs can experience a range of emotions, including happiness, anxiety, fear and anger. It's important to understand which emotions your dog is feeling so that you can take any action necessary to make sure they are happy and healthy.

Dogs communicate mainly through body language. They use different parts of their anatomy, including their tails, ears and eyes, to signal how they are feeling. All dogs are individuals, though, and will display differences in their behaviour. As they also come in many shapes and sizes, it can sometimes be difficult to read their body language and tell how they're feeling. For example, dogs with really short tails may not be able to lower them to signal that they're feeling worried. It's therefore important to spend time watching your dog in order to learn what is normal behaviour for them. You need to be able to understand the signals they're giving out.

Use the guide on the following pages to help identify important body language signals and get to know how your dog is feeling. If you're familiar with your dog's normal behaviour, it's then easy to spot any changes — and if you become aware of any alterations in your dog's behaviour, you should seek veterinary advice, as your dog may be distressed, bored, ill or injured.

▶

A happy dog

A dog that is happy will have a relaxed body posture, smooth fur, mouth open and relaxed, ears in a natural position, tail wagging, eyes normal shape. When it's inviting you to play it will have its bottom raised, smooth fur, high wagging tail, eyes normal shape, ears in a natural position and it may be barking excitedly. When standing, its weight will be distributed evenly across all four paws, smooth fur, tail wagging, face interested and alert, with a relaxed and open mouth.

A worried dog

These dogs are telling you that they are uncomfortable and don't want you to go near them. The dog may be standing but its body posture and head position will be low. Its tail will be tucked under, its ears will be drawn back and the dog will be yawning. The dog may be lying down avoiding eye contact or turning its head away from you, and licking its lips. Again, its ears will be drawn back. Alternatively, the dog may be sitting with its head lowered, ears back, tail tucked away, not making eye contact, yawning and raising a front paw.

An angry or very unhappy dog

A dog showing these behaviours will want you to stay away or go away. It may be standing with a stiffened body posture, weight forward, ears up, fur raised. It will be looking at you directly, its eyes with dark and enlarged

▶

pupils. Its tail will be up and stiff, its nose wrinkled. Alternatively, the dog may be lying down, cowering. Its ears will be flat, teeth bared, tail down between its legs. It might also be standing with its body down, its weight towards the back. Its head will be tilted upwards, mouth tight, lips drawn back, teeth exposed, eyes staring, ears back and down, snarling.

Acknowledgements

Transworld Publishers, Middlechild Productions and Motion Content Group are enormously grateful to Jean Ritchie. A huge thank you to Ben Clark and Julian Alexander from LAW and the wonderful team at Channel 5: Ben Frow, Lara Akeju, Sean Doyle and Greg Barnett. Many thanks also to all inspectors, staff and volunteers at the RSPCA. A final thanks must go to the owners of the wonderful dogs featured in these pages, who have given up their time to enable their beloved pets' stories to be included here.

Picture Acknowledgements

All photographs are courtesy of Middlechild Productions except where otherwise stated.

Timmy, p. 1 and picture section, courtesy of Jo Oultram; Lily, p. 39 and picture section, courtesy of John and Hazel Catt; Flint, p. 53 and picture section, courtesy of Mike Garnett; William, p. 127 and picture section, courtesy of Rachel Butler; Molly, p. 163 and picture section, courtesy of Amanda Hull; Buddy, p. 183 and picture section courtesy of Wendy Walters.